Howard D. Mehlinger

school reform in the information age

Center for Excellence in Education
Indiana University

Center for Excellence in Education (CEE)
Indiana University
Wendell W. Wright Education Building
201 North Rose Avenue
Bloomington, IN 47405-4006
Telephone (812) 856-8210; FAX (812) 856-8245;
E-Mail mehlinge@indiana.edu

Printed in the United States by Indiana University Printing Services

ISBN 0-9645857-0-7

Library of Congress
  Catalog card #: 95-92373

Sales and marketing inquiries should be directed to:

Media Management Services, Inc.
105 Terry Drive, Suite 120
Newtown, PA 18940-3425
Telephone 800-523-5948; FAX 215-579-8589

CONTENTS

PREFACE

I wrote this book for myself and others like me: people who are not technology experts but who appreciate the impact technology is having on American society and its potential to improve instruction; who are passionate about the importance of schooling and determined to improve the schools we have; who are weary of educational faddism; who want straight talk about the strength and weaknesses of schools; who believe the reforms that will make a difference are those that affect how teachers teach and children learn; and who, when referring to the importance of responding to individual differences among children, mean it and are not simply using words for political advantage.

This is not an academic book. It was written for adult Americans who are concerned about schools and may do something to improve the current situation once they understand it. I hope my readers include school board members and state legislators because they have the power to shape policies that influence the direction of school reform.

This is an opinionated book; I make no apology for this. After more than 40 years in the teaching profession, both in secondary schools and higher education, I have an idea or two about what works and am willing to share them without hesitation. Whether my opinions have merit or not is for the reader to decide.

My views resemble closely those of colleagues in the Indiana University Center for Excellence in Education, whose mission is to explore appropriate applications of technology in education. One strong belief we share is that while technology is not the solution to every problem confronting schools, we are unlikely to obtain the schools we want until we take greater advantage of the power of modern technology and its appeal to youth.

ACKNOWLEDGMENTS

I could not have written this book without the help of many others. First of all, colleagues within and outside of the Indiana University School of Education offered suggestions, provided reading materials, and read portions of the manuscript. My associates in the Center for Excellence in Education, especially B.J. Eib, Martin Siegel, and Gerald Sousa were important; not only did they share advice, criticism, and encouragement regarding the book, but they have also served as my mentors. What I think about technology is based largely on what I have learned from them. Jennifer Schatz, Kris Junik, and Sonny Kirkley provided research assistance; Martha Zuppann obtained permissions and pursued other details relating to publication.

I want to thank the cartoonists and illustrators who allowed me to reproduce their work in this book: George Abbott, Elizabeth Boling, Bo Brown, Brian Duffy, Sidney Harris, Patrick Oliphant, Joel Pett, and Michael Streff. Their humor adds meaning to the prose.

I am also grateful to those school officials and educational reformers who allowed me to visit their programs and who shared published and unpublished material about their work. The names of these people appear throughout the text.

The Spencer Foundation provided funds that allowed me to employ a library assistant, supported travel to model schools and technology conferences, and contributed to the book's publication. I could not have completed the task without the grant.

I owe a special debt to Alfred Gebert and Christine Matzner, two extraordinary Swiss friends and colleagues. They arranged for me to hide away as their guests in a Swiss chalet for two months during the summer of 1994, providing exactly the time and place I required to produce the first draft of the manuscript.

Eve Russell, my secretary, assumed responsibility for all of the jobs associated with moving an idea to a final product: handling correspondence, booking travel, producing draft copies, and many other duties that she has performed magnificently for me over the last two and one-half decades.

And, finally, I am grateful to my wife, Carolee Mehlinger, not only for tolerating the distractions and ignoring the clutter that accompany 18-month projects, but also for teaching herself word processing on a laptop computer in order that she could produce the first draft of the manuscript while we worked in Switzerland.

I could not have completed the book without the efforts of all of these people. Alas, I am solely responsible for any foolish conclusions or mistakes that the reader may encounter.

Chapter 1

VISION AND MISSION

Where there is no vision, the people perish.
Proverbs 29:18

Powerful visions can evoke equally powerful human responses. Biblical images of heaven and hell have inspired and frightened millions of people throughout the ages, leading to extraordinary commitments of time, talent, and material resources by devoted followers.

Secular visions can also be effective. Poets, philosophers, and politicians have offered images of desirable futures that have appealed to many. Karl Marx envisioned a world dominated by socialism, where each person would contribute his talent to society and receive according to his need; his vision has both attracted and repelled people for more than a century. Dr. Martin Luther King Jr. dreamed of a world in which black people and white people could live peaceably together; his visions inspired a generation of civil rights workers. Visionaries such as these are able to mobilize others who are willing to work tirelessly to make their dreams realities.

Visions also serve individuals. Athletes often imagine themselves performing a difficult feat—leaping to a record height, catching a football in the midst of defenders, skiing the giant slalom in record speed, or belting a home run—before they actually perform the act. The mental rehearsal of the performance appears to focus their energy and skill while inspiring self-confidence, thereby enabling them to make their best effort under enormous pressure.

Each of us can likely recall when a personal vision enabled us to overcome obstacles and achieve our goals. Perhaps it was when we were deciding on a career, pursuing our future spouse, or saving for a home; the vision of what we wanted led us to set priorities, work with exceptional energy, and live in accord with our highest principles; our vision also enabled us to persist despite stress, fatigue, and occasional disappointment.

The prophet was right: *Where there is no vision, the people perish.* He might have added: Where there is a vision, nearly anything is possible. What is a vision? While the term is employed variously, I am using the term vision to stand for a mental image of a desirable state of affairs. A vision statement provides a description of the kind of world we want. Vision statements are created for the purpose of inspiring and ennobling human activity. A vision can make ordinary tasks seem important. By setting direction, a vision statement helps set priorities and guides public policy.

A vision statement is not the same as a prediction. Vision statements set forth descriptions of a desirable future. Predictions of the future, often presented as scenarios, foretell what is likely to occur in the future if one or more current tendencies prevail. For example, given certain trends in American society, we could predict further growth of poverty among children and youth. Yet no one's vision of the future would suggest that one-third of American children *should* lack the basic necessities of daily life.

Predictions are often based on the assumption that human beings will not or cannot act in ways to change the direction of events. During earlier stages of human history, this might have been true; but it need not be true today. Within the physical limitations placed upon us by nature, we can create the future we want; but first we must have a vision that is worthy of our efforts.

What are the elements of a powerful, public vision? First of all, it must appeal to those beyond the visionary himself. Followers must agree that the visionary's future would be better than the present or the past. A vision should appeal to one's highest human instincts, calling forth, for example, altruism as opposed to selfishness. Certainly, visions of hell have scared some people into becoming Christians, but the more powerful appeal to followers has been the living example provided by Jesus Christ. President John F. Kennedy attracted old and young Americans to the Peace Corps because of the vision he had for how such an agency could provide positive, unselfish service to people of other nations. President Woodrow Wilson rallied support for American entry into World War I in order "to make the world safe for democracy." Thus, a powerful vision is one that draws people to a cause that they judge to be more important than what they are currently doing. Such a vision wins our allegiance and may even become part of our identity.

Secondly, a powerful vision must be achievable in a reasonable amount of time. I may envision travel in space to other galaxies; I also imagine our establishing permanent colonies on other planets. These activities may occur at some time in the future, but they do not capture my interest nor that of many others who are unlikely to live long enough to reap the benefits from the sacrifices such efforts would require.

Thirdly, and most important of all, a vision should take advantage of the opportunities the future will afford. When President Kennedy said we would land a man on the moon by the end of the 1960s, most of the necessary technology to achieve that task had not been invented; but it was reasonable to believe that by the time they were needed, they would be available. A vision of the future which is nothing more than an idealistic description of the present or the past may be valuable in some way or another, but it is not a vision.

Vision and American Schools

We lack a compelling vision for our public schools. The absence of such a vision is a threat to the success of all current school reforms.

We have many critics of current school practice, and a sufficient number of school reformers, but too few visionaries. Some of the school critics are justified in their criticism, but they offer few solutions. Several of the solutions offered by school reformers might work if given a chance, but what chance do they have when those who must carry out the reform remain unconvinced and uninspired and when the general public, who must pay for educational risk-taking, remains skeptical?

None of the existing visionaries has attracted a large following. Some so-called visionaries are not true visionaries at all; they either offer visions that seem unachievable or unworthy of sacrifice—e.g., abandoning public schools altogether—or they encourage "rear-vision," looking to the past, creating an idealized version of long ago, and grafting it onto present practice. Some appear to be oblivious to the changing nature of our society and how these changes will impact on schools in the future. For example, our education system has not yet adjusted to the fact that formal instruction can no longer end with graduation from high school or college. Americans require institutions that provide continuing education throughout a lifetime.

Except for religious institutions it would be hard to imagine an American institution more susceptible to a noble vision than our public schools. Many educators have become teachers because they thought teaching to be a worthy cause. Helping children reach their potential; making certain that each child has a chance to succeed in life despite race, social class, or ethnic background; preparing the next generation of American leaders: These are a few of the slogans that have been used by American public school teachers and administrators.

Today, while such slogans continue to be recognized, they have lost credibility. For example, we say that schools should help each child reach his or her unique potential, but this is not the way we organize instruction. Most teachers teach every child the same material in the same way, and measure each child's performance by the same standards. This approach seems fair somehow; no child is given special treatment or unfair advantage. Thus, teachers embrace the value of treating each child as a unique individual while instructing children as if they were virtually identical. Many teachers would eagerly embrace a vision that would permit them to merge their practice with their values.

The absence of a compelling vision has a number of negative consequences for education. One is the impact on teacher education. Teacher education departments and colleges are frequently criticized for failing to prepare teachers adequately. The criticism comes from the public as well as from their teacher college graduates. The lack of a credible vision contributes to a deplorable situation in many colleges and universities, where faculty in the sciences and humanities actively discourage their brightest students from becoming teachers, and where the faculty who offer professional education courses cannot agree among themselves on how teachers should be prepared. Some education professors believe their job is to equip new teachers with ideas and techniques for teaching individual subjects; others believe their job is to develop autonomous professionals who can carve out roles similar to university professors; a few believe their job is to prepare teachers to be critics of American society. There is no consensus about what schools could (should) become; hence there is no consensus about the direction and purpose of teacher education.

The lack of vision also hinders the school reform movement. There is an old saying that if you don't know where you are going, any road will get you there. For more than a decade we have been attempting to reform our schools. In 1983, the *Nation at Risk* report prompted reform initiatives that led to longer school days, longer school years, tests and career ladders for teachers, more testing for students, and more demanding high school graduation requirements. The assumption behind the report seemed to be that students were lazy and teachers were soft. By 1989 it was obvious that this reform had not worked, so without dismantling the first wave of reform, we started a second wave. The latter reform was based upon the assumption that schools lacked knowledge of what was expected of them. By establishing national goals and standards, students and teachers will know clearly what they are to accomplish and can be held accountable for the results. This effort has been endorsed by the president of the United States, the various state governors, business leaders, and leaders of several major foundations. It is a highly visible effort; there is no doubt that national goals and standards will be developed and approved. But will they result in better schooling?

The drive to establish national goals and standards seems intended to "nationalize" (not necessarily federalize) American education. While it is asserted that there will be no single national test or national curriculum, states are being urged to align their goals and standards with the national ones; local school districts are being asked to do the same. Meanwhile, textbook companies will develop new textbooks that will reflect the national goals and standards, as will test developers. Schools will be given choices about which textbooks to purchase and which assessment instruments to purchase, but it will not make much difference; if the plan works, they will all be aligned. Schools and teachers will therefore be made more accountable because everyone will be teaching essentially the same content, and the public will be better informed by the results of state and national tests.

There is undoubtedly a vision lurking behind the rhetoric of national goals and standards, but it is not one that its proponents wish to articulate clearly; it would resemble too closely the vision that has guided educational systems in authoritarian states, leading to practices we have abhorred in the past. Furthermore, Americans would recognize it as the ultimate challenge to local control of schools.

While the process of creating national goals and standards is underway, fierce debates are taking place regarding the content of the curriculum and about new roles for students and teachers in the instructional process. Advocates of new course content want to break down disciplinary boundaries and focus on the study of real-life problems that require knowledge that cuts across the disciplines. These and other advocates urge that topics be studied in depth, foregoing superficial coverage that leads to short-term memorization of names, dates, and places without learning much about any of them. Some reformers urge that the instructional process be turned on its head; teachers should act like coaches or advisers to students; meanwhile students, both individually and as members of groups, should become more active learners pursuing topics of interest to them. Learning should be assessed by means of exhibitions and portfolios, a radically different approach to the short-answer tests now popular in schools. The last thing these reformers want is curriculum alignment.

Both reform ideas are being advanced simultaneously, in some cases endorsed by the same individuals and organizations although they are patently contradictory—more of A means less of B. Indeed, in a few cases the same reformers are leading the charge in both movements, presumably with fingers crossed.

Again, if we knew what kinds of schools we wanted, we could choose our path more wisely.

Why is it so easy to find fault with schools or to propose solutions to well-recognized problems and yet so hard to develop a vision of what an ideal school or educational system should be? Finding fault is easy; all one needs is the result of one or more tests comparing student performance to students in the past, to students in another country, or to some ideal standard. Do you believe all students should know algebra? If so, give students a test on algebraic knowledge. The results may shock you; all students do not know algebra! The ones who will do best on an algebra test are those who are currently studying algebra or have just completed its study. Those who will do the worst will be those who have not taken the subject or who studied algebra a year or so earlier and have forgotten much of what they learned because they have had no opportunity to use algebra since taking the course. The obvious recommendation is that everyone should study more algebra; at least this is how the reform process works today.

It is much harder to create a persuasive vision of a new kind of school. First, as noted earlier, a vision should call forth our best human instincts. Being first in the world in algebra by the year 2000 or helping to save American business from foreign competition lacks nobility. Secondly, a vision should be achievable within a reasonable period of time. Thus far, no one has put forth an agenda of school reform that has the slightest chance of being successful by the year 2000, the date favored by most business and government leaders.

But it is the third element of the definition that is the toughest of all; a vision should have a future orientation. We are good at predicting the past but poor at envisioning the future. Some futurists, such as Alvin Toffler, John Naisbitt, and Marvin Cetron, seem remarkably prescient about the directions the world is going. While some of the trends they identify are only marginally relevant to education (e.g., further proliferation of nuclear weapons), others seem central to education's future (e.g., continuing increase in the number and sophistication of service sector jobs and the further erosion of low-skilled jobs in industrial manufacturing). The problem for school planners is how to sort through these general ideas and devise an educational program suitable for the future that can be sold convincingly to school patrons who are living in the present, whose only benchmarks are the schools they attended 20 or 30 years before, and who must pay the bill.

Technology and a Vision of Schooling

When thinking about schools of the future, it is difficult to imagine a vision of schooling that ignores the role that computers, video, and other technology will play in shaping our system of education. Can one imagine, for example, anyone developing a vision of the future of American transportation while overlooking the role of jet-propelled aircraft? Or what would we think of a vision of future communication that ignored digitized electronic media? Yet, ignoring modern technology is precisely what is occurring in the movement to reform schools. While there are a few books and articles that link technology to school reform, these were writ-

ENVISIONING THE SCHOOL OF THE FUTURE—

ten mainly by proponents of instructional technology. For the vast majority of school reformers, the role of technology is virtually ignored.

We have given a name to the age in which we live—the Information Age. Information has become the new source of wealth, replacing cheap energy and accessible raw materials that supported the Industrial Revolution. Those who know how to take advantage of information have become the "gold collar worker," the newest elite.

It is also a time of global communication and relatively inexpensive, rapid transportation, permitting multinational corporations to produce goods abroad and transport them for sale in the United States less expensively, in some cases, than to produce them here. Electronic communications permit managers to supervise production and marketing and to secure finance capital on a global basis. If the future requires that people be able to operate successfully in such an environment, how can any credible vision of future schooling ignore the tools and skills required to work in such settings?

These technologies also challenge the very nature of schooling. Technology can put learners in charge of their own learning. Learning can be done at home rather than at school. Indeed, many students now have greater access to computers and computerized information at home than they do at school. In the past no one would have said that the typical student had more books at home than were available in the school library. We know that students already spend more time watching television than attending classes. Today the media are far more significant conveyors of culture, challenging parents and schools for the cultivation of adolescent knowledge and attitudes. Most schools treat the media as the enemy rather than as a potential ally. How will schools be affected as more and more software becomes available to students in their homes? How should the existence of these and other technologies affect our vision of schools of the future?

We have scarcely begun to understand the role technology will play in schools of the future. The Business Roundtable has included technology as the ninth point of its *Essential Components of a Successful Education System*. Their ideas for how technology can be used to improve current school practice are well articulated, but they stop short of how school itself would be different if one took full advantage of technology and exploited all of the resources available to teachers and students. Technology is not merely another reform idea, like site-based management or ungraded elementary schools; it will force a reconsideration of the very nature of schooling itself. Thus, it must occupy a central role in creating a new vision for American schools.

What would schools be like if they were to take full advantage of technology? I shall not attempt to provide a full description, but here are some likely characteristics of schools in the year 2005:

- Americans will have abandoned the 180-day school year and adopted year-round schooling. They now attend classes about the same number of days each year as do German and Japanese students. Resistance to year-round schooling was broken once it was understood that no one would be forced to attend class every day. Teachers and students are able to schedule vacations according to their interests and needs. The kinds of activities scheduled at school also vary greatly throughout the year, allowing some time for individual and group work that can be done wherever a student can plug into his computer.

- The school day is also longer. Schools are open from 7:00 a.m. to 10:00 p.m. each week day, but few teachers or students are at school for more than six hours. Schools open early and close late because schools have become primary information sources for learners of all ages, and the community provides adults to maintain the facilities at all hours. For children who are left by parents when they go to work and picked up at the end of the work day, schools have special facilities where children can be accommodated and cared for, enabling them to relax and have fun while continuing to work in a secure learning environment.

- Many new school buildings have been built, and older buildings have been thoroughly renovated and modernized. It began to dawn on people about the middle of the 1990s, that the public schools were the most important public assets in the community. Once adults began to use them as learning centers, they insisted that the schools be well maintained and equipped with the most advanced technology. Schools have once again become community centers, as well as places for children during the day. Many adults enroll in courses preparing them with new job skills; some high school-age students as well as older students are taking college-credit courses using the school's distance learning technology.

- School is less a place than it is a concept in the minds of many. Of course, there are buildings called *schools* that are far better equipped than those in the past. These buildings offer laboratories and technology for training not available elsewhere. For example, many schools now have *sensoriums* that permit entire groups of students to have virtual reality experiences. In the sensorium, students can experience *mini worlds* such as sensing what it might be like to be a white corpuscle fighting disease within the body, or *macro worlds* in which one gains an impression of what it must have been like to be present at the time of the "big bang" when the universe was born. In sensoriums, students can simulate the hunting of the wooly mammoth in pre-historic Indiana or experience the lift-off of a space-ship. The software that drives the sensoriums is very expensive, so it is shared among schools. Because few communities have been able to provide every school with a sensorium, students now make field trips *to* schools (at least those with sensoriums) rather than *away* from school to find exciting learning.

- *School,* however, is more than a building. A student is *at school* whether working on an assignment at home, in the public library, or elsewhere. Once students log onto their computers, they are *at school,* even if they are traveling with their parents in another country. Before the technology revolution, people divided student work into *school work* and *homework.* This distinction has little meaning today, because students can communicate with colleagues and teachers at a distance almost as easily as if they were physically present in the school building. The information access and communications capability of the new technology also was the key to breaking-up lock-step instruction. Students are now largely free to move through the curriculum as rapidly as they wish, merely stopping from time-to-time to demonstrate to teachers, parents, and peers what they have learned.

Technology has also blurred the distinction between home schooling and the public schools. Many children, once instructed entirely at home, are taking some courses *at school from home* by means of technology.

- The textbook is no longer the focus of instruction. Because every student is given a computer that also acts as a multi-media communication device, students are no longer limited to the pre-screened and packaged information contained in traditional textbooks. Students search libraries and databases electronically to obtain the information they require—and they can do this from their homes or at school. The demise of the textbook has had a profound effect on how and what students learn. In the twentieth century, students were expected to memorize and recall information from their textbooks. Now, students are expected to seek out information, assemble it, make judgments about its quality, and present their findings to others.

- Courses have changed markedly since the 1990s. In the past, courses, especially from grades 7-12, were designed to be approximations of college courses, watered down to fit the age and capability of students. It finally dawned on people that there was little point to teaching watered-down college courses in high schools when more than 50 percent of high school graduates would attend college and take *real* college courses; an even greater impetus to change was the perception that the traditional curriculum lacked value for non-college-bound youth.

  Today's curriculum draws its content from the natural and physical sciences, mathematics, humanities, social sciences, and the arts, but the content is structured around interdisciplinary problems requiring student investigation. The result has been much greater student interest in their courses, resulting in much higher output of energy and greater retention of knowledge by students than schools in the early 1990s.

- Methods of teaching have also had to keep pace with new kinds of instructional materials. At one time, the teacher's job was to oversee the acquisition of finite bits of knowledge by students and account for their understanding and retention of this knowledge by employing examinations to gain evidence of success. Today's teachers are expected to assist students in defining problems for investigation, assist them in the search for data, and coach them in the presentation of their findings.

  As a result teaching has become both more challenging and attractive as a career. For the first time that anyone can recall, teaching has become the first field of choice for Phi Beta Kappa scholars. Perhaps, the appeal of teaching is a result of improved working conditions, access to technology, the recognition accorded to teachers, and the opportunity to continue to learn; it is hard to believe that in the 1980s, the best college students avoided teaching.

Teachers also have much better access to parents than they did in the 1990s. New teachers can scarcely believe that teachers did not always have telephones in their classrooms, equipped with voice mail and modems. They cannot imagine how teachers could have taught while being denied access to these simple technologies. Now, of course, each teacher has a computer at school and at home. They also have access to a technical support staff in their school to maintain the information systems.

Teachers know much more about their students than was once the case. Electronic records maintain complete files on each student from the time they enter the school system until the day they leave it. Thus, teachers are able to teach their students more successfully than when such information was lacking.

In the past, student academic records were primarily grades earned in individual courses. Today, student products, including exhibitions as well as anecdotal comments by teachers, are included as part of the student's academic record. None of this would have been possible prior to the use of electronic databases.

• Teacher education has also changed radically. At one time, those preparing to teach had little contact with students until their senior year. Today, most teacher candidates are assigned students to tutor as soon as they enter the teacher education program; their students are found in a variety of schools nationwide in order to give the teacher-in-training experience with students from diverse backgrounds. The college mentor and his or her students are connected electronically via desktop video, which permits the student and teacher-in-training to see one another while exchanging information. Teachers-in-training also use interactive video to *look in* on live classes, and they can discuss the lesson with the demonstration teacher, when the class is over. These experiences provide teachers-in-training with many models of instruction.

Professional development does not stop when a teacher takes a job. First of all, teachers have a range of *expert systems* available to them electronically. If they are facing a problem they cannot resolve, there are expert colleagues ready to help. Nor do teachers have to leave their schools to enroll in graduate credit courses or special workshops on topics important to them. Universities and other groups compete with each other to bring professional information to teachers at any time, at any place, and in whatever form they wish it to be delivered. These are some of the advantages that have followed the allocation of several cable channels to educational programming.

- The greatest change of all is that there has been a 180-degree turn in the attitudes people hold about the purpose of schools and about learning. In the past, school was a place where students acquired information that was unavailable elsewhere. This information was packaged in courses, and students were expected to demonstrate through examination that they had acquired most of it before they were permitted to advance with their class. It was further assumed that students had to be tricked or coerced into learning because the process was tedious and difficult.

The current assumption is that students want to learn and can learn if given proper assistance and direction. Further, students do not learn the same way, at the same time, and at the same pace; they also want to learn different things. Beyond providing core knowledge and skills that everyone needs to be successful in society, schools focus on assisting students in becoming more successful independent learners. Students graduate from high school at different ages, having completed different kinds of programs. None of this would have been possible before modern instructional technology.

Ideas like these are missing from the discourse of educational reform. Without them we are restricted to attempts to improve upon what we have always done.

Mission of American Schools

If a vision statement tells others the kind of school we want, a mission statement describes the school's business. In my opinion, the primary business of school is to help students acquire useful knowledge.

Providing for useful knowledge is not the only purpose for schools; many other activities are undertaken, although they are of secondary importance. Schools offer entertainment for the community through programs in athletics, drama, and music. Schools feed students and transport them from home to school and back. They provide secure day care for those parents who would not otherwise know where to send their children. Teachers serve as career counselors, coaches, and therapists in addition to their instructional duties.

Sometimes the secondary activities of schools seem to overshadow the more primary mission. In 1953, I signed a contract to teach history and serve

as assistant basketball and football coach in a small Kansas high school. The superintendent made clear to me that basketball was the community's top priority; therefore it was his as well. If, for example, the head coach felt the need for a special practice during the heart of the school day, he said the principal would ring a bell summoning the players from their classes to the gymnasium. Regular academic instruction would continue without the players.

The high school was located at one end of the main street in this small town with the post office at the opposite end. In between were drug stores, hardware stores, restaurants, and other small businesses. The superintendent said it was not unusual for the coach to begin at the post office at 8:00 a.m. on a Monday morning and devote nearly two hours walking the distance from the post office to the high school, only four to five blocks away. According to the superintendent, many merchants wanted to discuss the previous weekend's game and be given the opportunity to offer coaching advice. The most important thing the coach could do, in the superintendent's opinion, in addition to producing a winning team, was to keep the merchants happy by listening patiently to their suggestions. He noted that once, following a poor season, the school board decided change was needed. Not only was the coach fired, but the board fired nearly half of the high school faculty as well. Presumably, the teachers could not have been doing a good job if the team played so poorly.

It was clear to me that the primary mission of this small school was basketball, providing entertainment for the community. Fortunately, I was given an opportunity to withdraw from my contract in order to accept another job prior to the onset of the school year. While I never had the experience of teaching in this school, I followed its performance from a distance. It had great basketball teams, but little was heard of its best scholars.

While the example cited above may be extreme, it is so only in degree, not in direction. It is still the case in many American high schools that a school's reputation is known as much or more for its extracurricular program as for its academic one. Successful athletes are lionized by fellow students, the media, the community, and even the state legislature; it is more important in many schools to be a cheerleader than to be elected to the National Honor Society. Very bright, academically talented students frequently pretend to be average so as not to stand out and lose the respect of their peers. If these indicators are valid, helping students acquire knowledge—useful or otherwise—may not be the primary mission in some schools, but it should be.

Useful Knowledge

What is *useful knowledge?* Certainly knowledge implies more than information. Teachers may dispense hundreds of items of information and leave students without knowledge. Information is necessary but not sufficient for knowledge. Knowledge implies the ability to take in new information and organize it in a form that is useful to the learner. New information must be squared somehow with information already in hand. Knowledge becomes personal, unique to each individual. Students can be helped in building their knowledge; they cannot be given knowledge.

Knowledge is more easily acquired if it has value to the learner. We can memorize or repeat nonsense symbols for a short time, but they are rarely retained. They have no intrinsic value.

One reason schooling is boring for so many students is that they see little value in what they are asked to learn. Neither do many of their teachers as well, but someone *approved* the course, and it must be taught. As a result many students treat schooling as something to be endured; it is part of growing up, like having pimples. They act as if the purpose of learning is to perform on tests, in part because they see no other purpose. They take the tests and then promptly forget the data, as they are rarely asked to use the information again. Many do only what is necessary for getting by because they see no reason to work harder.

At the present time some reformers want schools to focus on *core knowledge.* Lists of names, dates, and events are compiled with suggestions for grade levels and courses where they can be taught. It is true that there is a kind of basic cultural literacy that must be mastered in order to engage in normal human discourse. Yet I remain skeptical of the value of most core knowledge proposals. The recommendations reflect too often the views of academicians. What they judge to be *core knowledge* is basic to their lives in the university; it is not clear that knowledge of Shakespeare, the Roman Empire, and the Renaissance are equally important to people in other occupations. Nor is it usually the case that the only opportunity to acquire such facts is in the public schools.

There are ways to make the academic knowledge interesting and vital to youth, but the pressure on schools to cover many topics, albeit superficially, inhibits sound instruction. Take the example of Julius Caesar and his decision to lead his army across the Rubicon River in 49 B.C. Typically, students will be asked to recall who (Julius Caesar), where (Rubicon) and when (49 B.C.). In contrast, the topic could be explored at length, yielding greater benefits to students. Teachers might ask: Why did Caesar challenge the Roman Senate? Are there ever justifications for such defiance? What was the ultimate effect on the Roman Republic? When students explore these latter questions in depth they gain more than an ability to recall discrete, unconnected data; they gain insights into leadership, corruption, and personal ambition: knowledge that might prove valuable over a lifetime. Students are not merely acquiring information, they are building a knowledge base they can use in future situations when encountering people with political ambition.

What makes some knowledge useful and other knowledge useless? This is not easy to answer because ultimately the decision about what is or is not valuable must be made by the learner. However, our inability to distinguish precisely between useful and useless knowledge for others cannot paralyze us, preventing us from making judgments or allowing the *status quo* to make the decision for us. Many of the topics we teach in school exist as a result of tradition, not because we can mount a plausible defense for their presence today. Other topics are included or excluded because of the influence by one or more special interest groups. For example, sound, sensible sex education, which could be enormously helpful to adolescent youth, is frequently denied them because the topic offends the sensitivities of one or more individuals in a community.

SCANS Report

In June 1991, the Secretary of Labor's Commission on Achieving Necessary Skills (SCANS) issued a report entitled, *What Work Requires of Schools: A SCANS Report on America 2000.*[1] The purpose of this report was to define the knowledge and skills judged to be most useful for the world of work. While the commission was primarily concerned about the K-12 schooling of students who do not attend college, the report offered recommendations that seem appropriate to all students.

The commission was created because the workplace has changed in recent years, because schools were being given conflicting advice regarding the kind of knowledge and skills adult workers needed to be successful employees, and because American employers were reporting difficulty in finding a sufficient number of qualified workers to meet their requirements. Thus, *useful knowledge,* from the point of view of the SCANS Report, is the knowledge, skills, and attitudes needed for employment. SCANS found that effective job performance has two elements: *competencies* and a *foundation.* The report identified five competencies and a three-part foundation of skills and personal qualities that are essential to the preparation of all youth, whether they are beginning work upon graduation from high school, attending college, or entering the armed services. The commission further agreed that the most effective way for students to learn these competencies and acquire the necessary foundation was in the context of learning within a real environment in which the skills were needed. In short, for students to learn them as abstract concepts to be applied later, would lead to poor results. Schools should teach the competencies and foundations because they are necessary for both schooling and work. What are these competencies and foundation?

Five Competencies[2]

Resources: Identifies, organizes, plans, and allocates resources

- A. *Time*—selects goal-relevant activities, ranks them, allocates time, and prepares and follows schedules
- B. *Money*—uses or prepares budgets, makes forecasts, keeps records, and makes adjustments to meet objectives
- C. *Material and Facilities*—acquires, stores, allocates, and uses materials or space efficiently
- D. *Human Resources*—assesses skills and distributes work accordingly, evaluates performance and provides feedback

Interpersonal: Works with others

- A. *Participates as Member of a Team*—contributes to group effort
- B. *Teaches Others New Skills*
- C. *Serves Clients/Customers*—works to satisfy customers' expectations
- D. *Exercises Leadership*—communicates ideas to justify position, persuades and convinces others, responsibly challenges existing procedures and policies

E. *Negotiates*—works toward agreements involving exchange of resources, resolves divergent interests

F. *Works with Diversity*—works well with men and women from diverse backgrounds

Information: Acquires and uses information

A. *Acquires and Evaluates Information*

B. *Organizes and Maintains Information*

C. *Interprets and Communicates Information*

D. *Uses Computers to Process Information*

Systems: Understands complex interrelationships

A. *Understands Systems*—knows how social, organizational, and technological systems work and operates effectively with them

B. *Monitors and Corrects Performance*—distinguishes trends, predicts impacts on system operations, diagnoses deviations in systems' performance and corrects malfunctions

C. *Improves or Designs Systems*—suggests modifications to existing systems and develops new or alternative systems to improve performance

Technology: Works with a variety of technologies

A. *Selects Technology*—chooses procedures, tools, or equipment, including computers and related technologies

B. *Applies Technology to Tasks*—understands overall intent and proper procedures for setup and operation of equipment

C. *Maintains and Troubleshoots Equipment*—prevents, identifies, or solves problems with equipment, including computers and other technologies

It is obvious that the actual performance of these competencies will vary depending upon the nature of the task. The way a chef in a hotel kitchen organizes *resources* is quite different from the way a merchant operates a store, but both need the skill of using resources competently. While schools can and should contribute to building each competency in a general way, the technical application of each competence has to be learned on the job.

These competencies should be built upon a three-part foundation of skills and attitudes. Without this foundation, they are less likely to be achieved.

A Three-Part Foundation[3]

Basic Skills: Reads, writes, performs arithmetic and mathematical operations, listens and speaks

A. *Reading*—locates, understands, and interprets written information in prose and in documents such as manuals, graphs, and schedules

B. *Writing*—communicates thoughts, ideas, information, and messages in writing; and creates documents such as letters, directions, manuals, reports, graphs, and flow charts

C. *Arithmetic/Mathematics*—performs basic computations and approaches practical problems by choosing appropriately from a variety of mathematical techniques

D. *Listening*—receives, attends to, interprets, and responds to verbal messages and other cues

E. *Speaking*—organizes ideas and communicates orally

Thinking Skills: Thinks creatively, makes decisions, solves problems, visualizes, knows how to learn, and reasons

A. *Creative Thinking*—generates new ideas

B. *Decision Making*—specifies goals and constraints, generates alternatives, considers risks, and evaluates and chooses best alternative

C. *Problem Solving*—recognizes problems and devises and implements plan of action

D. *Seeing Things in the Mind's Eye*—organizes, and processes symbols, pictures, graphs, objects, and other information

E. *Knowing How to Learn*—uses efficient learning techniques to acquire and apply new knowledge and skills

F. *Reasoning*—discovers a rule or principle underlying the relationship between two or more objects and applies it when solving a problem

Personal Qualities: Displays responsibility, self-esteem, sociability, self-management, and integrity

A. *Responsibility*—exerts a high level of effort and perseveres towards goal attainment

B. *Self-Esteem*—believes in own self-worth and maintains a positive view of self

C. *Sociability*—demonstrates understanding, friendliness, adaptability, empathy, and politeness in group settings

D. *Self-Management*—assesses self accurately, sets personal goals, monitors progress, and exhibits self-control

E. *Integrity/Honesty*—chooses ethical courses of action

While schools have traditionally been responsible for *basic skills*, SCANS concluded that less than half of young adults had achieved the level of skill required to operate successfully in the modern workplace. *Thinking skills* have also been part of the school's responsibility, but they have often been given secondary priority to *basic skills*. The development of *personal qualities* has been a shared responsibility between home and school. Without fixing blame, employers often complain that these five personal qualities are missing in the people they hire, and they hold the schools accountable for their absence.

According to SCANS, all people require these five competencies and the three-part foundation. To SCANS, this is the most *useful knowledge* students can acquire in school.

Robert Reich, the U.S. Secretary of Labor, has offered his opinion about what knowledge is most useful. In his book, *The Work of Nations,* he identified four basic *skills* as fundamental to the education of American youth: *abstraction, system thinking, experimentation, and collaboration.*[4]

Abstraction stands for the capacity to apply meaning to the jumble of activities going on around a person. Some people, because of their education, see patterns of meaning in events, while others see little or nothing at all. I recall many years ago the pride that a colleague and anthropologist showed in his eighth-grade daughter who was using an experimental course called *American Political Behavior,* designed for use in junior high and high school civics and American government courses. One of the key concepts in the course was *political socialization,* the process by which people become indoctrinated into a particular political culture. He reported to me that he had taken his daughter and some of her friends to a basketball game. As they stood, prior to the start of the game, having risen to attention with the first bars of the "Star Spangled Banner," my colleague heard his daughter whisper to her friend: "Do you know why we are standing? Political socialization!"

Some may think it is vital that children remember such facts as who wrote the national anthem, on what date, and because of which assault on what fort. I, and presumably Reich, would settle for the capacity exhibited by the eighth-grade student: an ability to reflect on and draw meaning from events that are treated as routine by others.

System thinking carries abstraction to a higher level. Information is generally presented to school students as discrete parts of courses, bits of data that may be intrinsically interesting but leave the student thinking the world consists of isolated objects unconnected to one another. This is not true in the real world. Issues are rarely isolated and disconnected to other phenomena. The world operates in systemic ways with one thing acting on another: Solve one problem and another unanticipated outcome appears. Thus, students need to learn to see connections and relationships across topics.

Experimentation need not be the kind one expects to encounter in science classrooms, although such experiments play an important role in schooling. Experimentation also stands for more modest explorations in which students conduct their own inquiries, try out their own ideas, learn by trial and error. Learning outside of school is often performed this way; we try to do something, fail, try again, fail and finally succeed. Typical school learning is just the opposite. Too little time is allowed for student exploration; more topics, treated superficially, rather than fewer topics studied in depth is generally the rule.

The fourth skill is the ability to *collaborate*. Most school time is focused on individual learning rather than group learning. Students are discouraged from sharing ideas or working together on projects. In school we call collaboration cheating; in the adult world it is called team work.

Except in the very best schools that attract the academic elite, none of the four skills identified by Reich is emphasized in American public schools. They do not appear on most lists of core knowledge yet they are fundamental for successful work in the modern age.

It may be that the most useful knowledge a student can acquire is knowledge about how to become a self-learner, a continuous learner, a joyful learner. And possibly the most mischievous message our educational system conveys is that at the end of high school or upon graduation from college one is *educated*. One has learned all one needs to know.

Today there are no learned people, only the learning and the slipping out-of-date.

Technology and School Mission

Many educators, public officials, and business leaders believe that knowledge of technology has become useful. Nearly every school has at least one computer, and courses aimed at providing computer literacy have appeared in schools across the country. In the minds of some, courses on computers are the equivalents of courses in driver education. They argue that because every one is likely to use a computer someday, it is important that schools teach students how to operate them. This opinion is important but not sufficient and points to a misunderstanding of the role modern technologies play in our society. After all, we do not learn to drive cars for the goal of driving cars. We want to drive cars in order to reach destinations that are important to us. We need to use technology because it helps us accomplish tasks that are important to us.

Computers and other electronic tools have altered the role of information in our lives. Much of the information we now receive has been selected and digested for us. Newspapers, for example, reflect decisions by editors about what they think we want to read; the final product is a result of prior screening of hundreds of stories before choosing the ones to be printed. Electronic newspapers provide a greater opportunity for readers to make their own selections. We can read many more articles on any given topic than a typical newspaper will choose to print.

Computers and other tools also provide access to libraries and archives worldwide. Students need not be contented with the information in their textbooks; they can peek behind the generalizations to study the evidence used by the authors.

At one time, the school's mission was to be a primary source of information. Today, schools must help students learn how to acquire, select, evaluate, analyze, synthesize, and apply information. Students must master technology in order to perform these tasks.

Television has become one of the principal sources of information for children and adults. Students need to understand how television works, how to use it, and how to defend themselves when it is employed by others. It is futile for schools to resist television; they should be taking the mystery out of it and helping students use it to their advantage.

Conclusion

We are products of our experience. We understand the world as we were taught to interpret it and have experienced it ourselves. Most adult Americans have school experience: They attended one and they have sent their children to school. Whether their experience was pleasant or unpleasant, they think they know what a school is and they judge reform proposals according to whether they make sense or not, based on their understanding of school. When we understand that schools serve a conservation function in our culture rather than a transforming one, it is easy to see why our visions of school are so limited and why schools find it so hard to change.

While all this is true, schools will change because our society is changing. While schools may not lead in the transformation of culture, neither can they lag far behind it.

Information Age technology is the single greatest factor affecting the ways we live; it cannot help but alter the way we conduct schooling. We need to imagine what schools would be like that took full advantage of technology and take the steps necessary to create such schools. No single person or group has yet produced a compelling vision of schools utilizing technology fully and appropriately, yet we need such visions now.

The mission of schools, providing students with useful knowledge, is unlikely to change. But the definition of useful knowledge will surely change dramatically when we fully appreciate what students need to gain from school in order to be successful. When we understand that the results of schooling must be different, we may then be ready to consider more radical changes in curricula, teaching methodologies, and the structure of schooling.

Technology is the key to a new school vision and a revised mission. It is not that we should worship technology anymore than astronauts worship rocket boosters. Technology is important only to the degree that it helps us get where we want to go. If we have a vision of schooling that calls for students to work to their capacity, at their own pace, at tasks they find to be challenging and enjoyable, we are likely to be successful only if we take advantage of the opportunities afforded us by new technologies.

Chapter 2

SCHOOL REFORM—AGAIN? FINALLY?

A nation cannot have a first-place economy with a second-rate education system.
William J. Kohlberg and Foster C. Smith[1]

We are in the midst of another effort to reform American schools. If you make your living as an educator, this is hardly news. We are always responding to one reform proposal or another. Skeptics believe this reform will pass too, to be followed in another decade by another round of suggestions. The proponents of the current reform effort believe this one is different: This time the ideas are more comprehensive; this reform has broader public support; this reform will change schools.

School reforms always require some larger social justification. We seem incapable of reforming schools for the purpose of improving conditions for students and teachers. Our reforms must be aimed at maintaining national defense, beating the Russians to the moon, fighting poverty, or overcoming racism. This time we must reform schools to improve our competitive position with economic rivals, especially Germany and Japan, and to maintain our standard of living.

We seem driven first to assign blame to schools for whatever social problem we face, and then turn to the schools to save us. Using schools as scapegoats for flawed business or government policy is unfair; counting on schools to solve problems beyond their mission is silly. It merely sets up schools for further failure.

In the quotation above, Kohlberg and Smith imply that we do not now—or will soon not—have a first-place economy and that this problem is somehow the result of a second-rate education system. We should assume, logically, that when the United States was indisputably the world economic leader it was because we had undeniably the world's best educational system. I don't recall this ever being said by business or government leaders.

If we did have a second-rate educational system, how would we know? If we were to ask the American public for its opinion about the quality of our schools, as the Gallup Poll has done for Phi Delta Kappa on an annual basis since 1969, their answer would be confusing. In the 1994 poll,[2] when people were asked to assign letter grades to the quality of schools, 70 percent gave a grade of A or B and 92 percent gave a grade of at least C to the schools attended by their eldest child, while the nation's schools as a whole received much lower grades; only 22 percent thought schools deserved an A or B, while only 49 percent gave a grade of at least a C. When assigning grades to those schools in their community, 44 percent gave local schools a grade of A or B; 74 percent thought they deserved a C or better; only 7 percent assigned an F. How can this be? If most people believe the school their child attends is satisfactory, why do they think schools as a whole are poor?

The inconsistency in the data is probably a result of Americans having been persuaded by media reporting that some schools, especially urban schools, are in miserable shape. We are saturated with problem stories about inner-city schools. Except for those Americans who send their children to inner-city schools, we depend upon the media to tell us what is happening in those schools. But with regard to our own schools—where we went to school, where we send our children or grandchildren for instruction, where we know one or more teachers, even the principal or superintendent—those schools are fine. Americans believe that their own schools are doing what is expected of them. Are they wrong?

To counteract American apathy about their schools, critics frequently draw upon published results of Scholastic Aptitude Test (SAT) scores, achievement tests, international examinations and other indicators for evidence that schools compare unfavorably with those in the past, with schools in other countries, or with what the critics believe to be expected performance. For example, in April 1994, the National Education Commission on Time and Learning reported that during the last four years of secondary school, American high school students devote much less time to academic subjects than their counterparts in Japan, France, and Germany.[3] According to the commission report, *Prisoners of Time,* American students spent 1,460 hours on average over four years studying such subjects as mathematics, science, and history, while Japanese, French, and German students devoted 3,170, 3,280, and 3,528 hours respectively to their study. In short, American students spend less than half the time on these subjects than do students in countries that are our economic rivals.

What are American students doing with their time? Some is devoted to subjects such as driver's education, health, safety, conservation and energy, family life, AIDS, and other nonacademic subjects. Although a typical American school day is six hours, the commission estimated that only three and one-half hours are devoted to academic subjects; the remainder of the time is given to study hall, homeroom, extracurricular activities, assemblies, and nonacademic courses. American students also devote less time to homework. For example, approximately one-half of all Japanese secondary school students are enrolled in *Juku* schools—private, tutorial services that enrich instruction, offer remedial help, and prepare Japanese students for university examinations. In Germany and France, students on average spend more time on homework and watch less television than do American students. American students also spend an average of 180 days each year attending school. The number climbs to 180-200 for French students, 220-226 for German students, and 230 for Japanese students.

It is likely American students would do better in academic subjects if more time were devoted to their study. These matters are decided by others, always adults and usually state government officials, the same people who are critical of schools. Presumably, those Americans who like schools as they are remain content with the existing curriculum and with the current length of the school year. Yet they wish to compare the results of the academic performance of American students with those in countries who provide twice the opportunity to master academic subject matter.

Most critics of American schools believe that our schools not only compare unfavorably with our economic rivals—mainly Germany and Japan—they are also no longer as good as they once were. In short, American kids are dumber and their teachers less dedicated, able, and ambitious than was once the case. Is this true?

Again, it is difficult to be certain. While many Americans have been led to believe that American schools in general are not as good as they were in the past, one recent study drew contrary conclusions. I am citing this study in particular because it was carefully done, because the investigators had no reason to make the schools look better or worse than they are, and because of the knowledge and skill of the investigators. The researchers, C. C. Carson, R. M. Huelskamp, and T. D. Woodall, are scientists employed in the Strategic Studies Center of Sandia National Laboratories, one of the high energy labs operated for the U.S. Department of Energy. Responding in part to President George Bush's request that various departments of the federal government seek ways to help strengthen American education, these three scientists undertook a comprehensive study of American education, focusing especially on the high school grades. The purpose of their study was to gain an accurate picture of the actual condition of American schools in order that the Sandia National Laboratories could plan an appropriate intervention.

The Sandia study is interesting in part because their findings contradicted other evidence used by the U.S. Department of Education and the White

House to justify federal education policy. The challenge posed by the report led some high government officials to attempt to bury it, and they ordered the scientists not to publish their findings. Although portions of the report leaked and were widely discussed among educators in 1991 and 1992, a published version did not appear until 1993.[4]

The study reached interesting conclusions about the status of American schools. For example, one indicator commonly used to note the decline of American schools has been published SAT results, a test typically taken by high school seniors for the purpose of providing information to college admission officers regarding their ability to perform well in college. The Sandia study confirmed that SAT scores had indeed declined about 5 percent over the preceding 20 years, but following some decline in the 1970s, every subgroup taking the SAT since 1975 had shown improvement. Further, the decline in the SAT scores was attributed by the investigators mainly to the increasing number of students taking the test. A greater portion of tests takers was being drawn from students who performed at an average or lower level in school courses, those who in the past would not have expected to go to college but now intended to do so. Thus, instead of using the SAT decline as a negative indicator, the Sandia researchers reported, ". . . the decline in average SAT scores can be construed as a positive sign indicating that a larger portion of high school graduates is availing itself of the opportunity to pursue a college education." They also concluded that "student performance data clearly indicates that today's youth are achieving levels of education at least as high as any previous generation."

Critics of American schools have also pointed to the "high" dropout rates among high school students. The Sandia study found that on-time graduation rates had remained relatively steady at 75 percent since 1965. If the GED[5] is included, the high school completion rate is over 85 percent. The Sandia data took into account all 17-year-old American residents, including recent immigrants. Many immigrants are young adults who are unlikely ever to *drop in* to a traditional American high school but they are counted as dropouts because they lack a high school diploma. Across all of the various subgroups, the dropout rate was highest for Hispanics; the lowest by far was the 6.8 percent dropout rate represented by blacks living in the suburbs. Given the heterogeneous nature of the American population, the investigators concluded that a much higher on-time graduation rate was not likely possible. They pointed out that Japan has an on-time graduation rate of 87 percent to 88 percent, but it has a much more homogeneous population and places much greater stress on education generally than does American society.

The Sandia scientists found that Americans continue to compare unfavorably with students of other countries in the areas of science and mathematics, in part for reasons noted earlier by the *Prisoners of Time* report. On the other hand, only Belgium and Finland had higher proportions of 17-year-olds in school; the United States leads the world in the percentage of young people obtaining bachelor's degrees and the percentage of degrees obtained by women and minorities. And while the U.S. lags behind other countries in certain specialties, the overall technical and nontechnical degree attainment by the American workforce and the population as a whole is unparalleled in the world.

The Sandia investigators discovered that very few employers seemed concerned about the lack of academic skills of their new employees; they were more upset about deficiencies in personal and social attributes: personal appearance, punctuality, absenteeism; these traits are not typically the focus of school instruction. In contrast to what has been frequently claimed, most employers were not investing money in remedial education for new employees to overcome deficient K-12 instruction. Ninety percent of private enterprise training dollars was being spent on college-educated employees (i.e., management rather than unskilled labor) and skilled laborers. What basic skills training existed that might have been classified as remedial was directed to older workers, long-term employees, who needed to improve their knowledge to fill positions requiring greater skills. These older employees are not products of the current school system but of the previous system that is often claimed to be superior.

What does this mean? If the Sandia study is credible, there is no *crisis* in American education; or, if there is a *crisis* it is not a result of the decline in the quality of American schooling overall. There is no doubt that some American school systems face very serious problems; the worst problems occur in some inner cities; others are found in rural areas and on Indian reservations. The vast majority of these problems are linked closely to social pathologies of American life: poverty, crime, drugs and alcohol, broken homes. For example, the number of children living in poverty has grown steadily to nearly 25 percent, more than double that of any other major industrialized nation. By eighth grade, 7 out of 10 children have consumed alcohol. Eleven percent of all American females age 15 to 19 become pregnant in any given year, double that of England, Wales, and Canada; nearly 4,000 children are murdered each year. The problems children face outside of school affect greatly their performance within school. If America's poor children could be provided the same conditions for growing up, including the same quality of schools, as those afforded to middle-class, suburban youth, we would have no crisis at all—at least as the crisis has been portrayed to date.

What is going on? Why are politicians and business leaders beating up on schools when the solutions to problems in education lie in curing problems associated with poverty and equitable funding of schools? The cynics say it is easier for business and political leaders to blame schools than it is to solve more significant problems associated with poverty. Probably some officials who speak confidently about the status of American education simply do not know better; they have relied too heavily on the views of those they respect and merely parrot what has become the accepted point of view.[6] It is also true that some firms, threatened with fierce international competition, may find it convenient to relieve some of their frustration by blaming others. If they elect to move a factory overseas to obtain cheaper labor, thereby causing a sharp drop in employment within a community, they can defend their action by claiming the schools do not provide graduates with adequate skills. It is also safer for public officials to join the attack on the schools than to criticize powerful industry officials.

Nevertheless, it is undoubtedly true that with more high school graduates choosing to attend college, there is a smaller pool of high school graduates available for full-time employment; it is also true that schools have higher portions of students who are recent immigrants, who arrive with little English and frequently poor academic backgrounds, and that these are often the people employers must rely upon; and finally, it is also true that the more our economy becomes a service economy and industrial jobs depend upon advanced technology, the intellectual demands on the labor force will increase. Schools, at least in some parts of the United States, may not be able to meet the local demand for highly-skilled graduates ready to enter the workforce upon high school graduation.

While there is validity in all of these arguments, they have been distorted and exaggerated to give a false picture of American schooling today. There is a crisis of sorts, but it is not the one simplistically portrayed. Schools are not shirking their responsibilities; kids are not dumber; teachers as a group are not sloughing off. Schools are providing the kind of education that we have asked them to provide for the last 100 years or so, and they are doing as well or better at that job than they have ever done, while working under much more difficult social conditions. Little wonder that teachers and school administrators are defensive and angry. They have a right to be. They are unjustifiably blamed for school deficiencies that do not exist, for failing to solve social problems outside their control, and for conducting schooling in accord with community expectations.

The challenge we face is how to reform a highly successful school system, one that has served Americans well for more than a century, into a new kind of system that is more in tune with current needs. Schools are caught in a process of social change that is transforming most sectors of American society. Some of the sectors have not coped with change as well as schools have, but we have not blamed them for failing. For example, we do not attribute the decline of central cities and the rise of shopping malls to laziness on the part of downtown merchants. They were influenced by the desire of middle class Americans to move from the city to the suburbs and to shop closer to where they lived. Large retail chain stores have emerged to satisfy the desire of Americans for mall shopping. Such stores buy in large quantities and offer more goods at lower prices than the small one owner shops can do. We may regret the decay of small towns and central cities and abhor the spread of commercial malls, but we like the convenience of mall shopping. We also understand that our attitudes are largely responsible for the results.

The world has changed for American schools as well; some of the changes have occurred so slowly that they have scarcely been noticed by the general public. For example, consider local control of schools. This long-cherished idea in American education has set us apart from most systems of schooling around the world, where teachers are national civil servants and schools are operated by the national ministry of education. According to the U.S. Constitution, education was left to the states; the states in turn delegated most of their authority—and the responsibility to fund schools—to local communities. Local authorities once ran the schools; but this is no longer true. Thus, we are experiencing conceptual lag; our terms—e.g., *local control*—prevent us from seeing the situation that actually exists.

It is no longer possible to run a school system and respond only to local needs. While local boards of education still control some matters, such as selecting the superintendent and deciding on the school budget, assignment of pupils is heavily influenced by federal law and decisions by federal and state courts; the curriculum is determined largely by state departments of education; what is taught in classes is influenced by available textbooks designed to serve a national market; and teacher recruitment and retention policies are circumscribed by state law and negotiated with teacher unions that follow state and national guidelines set by their organizations. As states move to take over a greater share of the cost of operating public schools, legislatures want a large voice in how the money is spent. Only 25 years ago, it would have been unthinkable for a president of the United States to join with the 50 governors to establish national goals for education; today, it seems reasonable and appropriate to most Americans that they do so.

While the erosion of local control has been underway for a long time, Americans still believe that their school, their school system, should respond to their ideas. If you doubt my opinion, let some congressman propose a national curriculum on values education and wait for the reaction.

It will not be easy to change the American system of public education with its 15,000 separate school districts, 85,000 different schools, and 2,450,000 teachers, especially when school officials and most Americans are unsure that major change is needed or desirable. In our personal lives we do not choose radical solutions to problems when patience and enough time may permit the problem to take care of itself. Who, for example, would elect surgery to remove a tumor if it might disappear on its own or be reduced by taking pills?

Although some critics believe that the very survival of public schools is at stake, most Americans do not have the same sense of urgency. They cannot imagine a time when there would be no public schools; they believe that any problems schools are facing can be fixed. The likelihood of major change is further undermined by lack of agreement among experts on what solutions are required and what schools should become.

A few believe that schools are incapable of changing to a necessary degree so long as they remain public institutions. According to John E. Chubb and Terry M. Moe, "Democratic control normally produces ineffective schools."[7] They believe that existing institutions—school boards, state legislatures, governors, Congress, the president—cannot solve school problems because *they* are the major source of the problem. Under the current system schools cannot respond directly to the needs of their clients, students, and parents, because they are agents of a society that is made up of many constituencies with ideas and concerns about education. The job of democratic institutions is to find a consensus among the contending parties; such consensus inevitably denies students and parents the best education possible. Chubb and Moe, and others like them, believe the way to have better schools is to let the market respond, putting public funds into the hands of students and parents and allowing them to purchase the education they want.

Much more could be said, both pro and con, about the advantages that might follow if public funds were to become available, permitting parents to select private schools for the education of their children. It is not my purpose to conduct that debate, useful as it might be. I only wish to acknowledge that a growing number of people see so little hope in the ability of schools to respond adequately to the changes occurring in our society that they are prepared to abandon them altogether.

Having set the stage, let us now turn to what various critics find wrong with schools and how they propose to change them.

Complaints and Solutions

Schools are criticized for not keeping greater portions of students in schools, for not providing a more demanding curriculum for those who are planning to attend college, for not preparing adequately for work those who do not go to college, for not providing safe conditions for students to study and so on. There is no single problem; neither is there a single reform plan on the table. There are many plans, and some are contradictory to one another.

I will not attempt to air all complaints; rather I will focus on features of schooling that seem to be at the heart of the problem, as judged by most critics. And, I will not review all of the reform proposals; that would be another book, and good sources are currently in print. I have no wish to duplicate published analyses of various reform efforts. My purpose here is to pinpoint why particular schemes are advanced and what the consequences might be of adopting one solution over another.

I have grouped the advocates into two camps: the top-down approach, favored by political and business leaders, and the bottom-up approach, favored by most education reformers. I am aware that such a distinction exaggerates the differences to a degree, and I know some reformers will be upset by being placed into a group according to such a distinction. Nevertheless, this grouping helps me understand the current reform process; it may also prove useful to the reader.

I have also selected one person or organization as largely representative of the top-down or bottom-up approach, even though I am aware that no single person or group can possibly represent all of the views and perspectives of others. My purpose is to understand a process underway, not to analyze all of the reform suggestions. Nor am I trying to single out one person or another as the leader.

Finally, I have chosen to include the views of students, teachers, and school administrators—the objects of the reform—separately. I am aware that the reformers believe that they represent those on the inside of schools, and surely some do to one degree or another. I cannot be confident that I can represent the diverse views of students, teachers, and school administrators from all parts of the country. Nevertheless, I think it is important to recognize that the objects of the reform process have opinions also about what is right and wrong about schools and what should be done to improve them. Their opinions as a group differ substantially from those of outsiders.

What is Wrong with American Schools?

The most simple way to sum up criticism is to say that the school system we have, which was designed for another age, does not perform well under current circumstances. Our school system was designed to provide a general education for the masses. It replaced a system that once provided primary education for many, and a highly academic secondary school program leading to college for a tiny elite. This system functioned well during most of the twentieth century, and for a part of that time it was admired and copied by other nations. The fact that it was once judged to be very successful has led people to want to address specific weaknesses rather than confront the possible need for an entirely new system.

The public education system we know today did not fully materialize until the beginning of this century. In colonial times and until the middle of the nineteenth century, few Americans had access to or took advantage of formal education. Only wealthy people could afford tutors and pay tuition to residential schools that would give children the instruction required for college admission and careers as members of professions, literati, and the governing class. Farmers and tradesmen, who comprised the vast majority of the population, needed to be able to read a little, write a bit, and compute well enough to transact business; but they had few aspirations beyond these levels. What schooling was required could be done at home and in church school.

All of this changed in the late nineteenth and early twentieth century. Urbanization and industrialization attracted vast numbers of immigrants to America. They needed to be socialized as citizens; they also needed rudimentary knowledge and skills to find jobs. The advent of child labor laws and compulsory school attendance laws, together with favorable court decisions that allowed public funds to be spent on public education, led to the growth of strong public schools.

This period also coincided with the rapid industrialization of the United States. In 1870, Germany and Great Britain were the undisputed world economic powers; 50 years later America had become the industrial leader. Certainly World War I contributed enormously to the redistribution of economic power, but the way in which American industry organized itself for production also made a difference.

The key for the manufacturing industry was mass production using technology, assembly line processes, and unskilled labor. The effect can best be seen in the automobile industry. Prior to Henry Ford, cars were largely hand-crafted, much as racing cars are today. This meant few could be produced, and they were very expensive, affordable only to very wealthy people. Henry Ford recognized that if cars could be produced cheaply, more people could buy them, leading to much greater profits. The problem was how to produce cars efficiently at the least possible cost.

The key cost variable was labor. While the cost of raw materials per car might not vary greatly, the time required to build a single automobile led to enormous variability on the cost of labor. The use of technology and the assembly line process made it possible to break tasks down to a very simple, repetitive act that unskilled laborers could perform; thus it was unnecessary to hire skilled craftsmen. Unskilled laborers could be paid much less and the pool of immigrant workers and displaced farm workers was adequate to the need.

The guru of mass production methods was Frederick W. Taylor, who in 1911 published *The Principles of Scientific Management*. Taylor's idea was to keep assembly line tasks simple as possible so that even the most illiterate person could do them. The tasks would be repeated hundreds of times each day, making the job so routine that the worker would scarcely need to think about it. While their job would certainly become boring, the workers would be grateful for their jobs if they were adequately paid; furthermore, they could *think* when they were off the job. Thinking on the job, said Taylor, was to be in the hands of management: managers, supervisors, planners, engineers, marketing specialists, etc. The *big thinker* was the president and CEO; his thinking was passed down through the firm's bureaucracy until it reached the front-line worker in terms of detailed instructions regarding how each production task was to be performed.

The system worked so well in industry that schooling was shaped to fit the industrial model. Franklin Bobbitt, an instructor at the University of Chicago, was among those educators who applied Taylor's ideas to schools. The key was to specify exactly what should be taught at each grade level, provide teachers with the equipment and supplies necessary for instruction, and then carefully supervise the teachers' performance. Children would proceed down the "assembly line" of K-12 education with each teacher filling them with the facts required for that grade level or subject area. At the end of 12 years, they would be fully educated—full of the facts they would need to begin college or become adult workers.

Perhaps the best expression of this idea was provided by the educator Elwood P. Cubberly, who in the 1930s wrote: "The public schools of the United States are, in a sense, a manufactory, doing a two-billion dollar business each year in trying to prepare future citizens for usefulness and efficiency in life. As such, we have recently been engaged in revising our manufacturing specifications and in applying to the conduct of the business some of the same principles of specialized production and manufacturing efficiency which control in other parts of the manufacturing world."[8]

To perform this task, schools needed docile, semieducated workers willing to work at low wages and to follow orders. They found them in women, for whom teaching was then practically the only available professional career, except for nursing. While many female teachers initially had little more education than the students they taught, it was judged sufficient as long as they had adequate supervision. In addition, women were thought to be especially good at *nurturing* children. Men took jobs as supervisors. They made all of the *important* decisions; they chose the textbooks, hired the staff, fixed the budget, assigned the students, communicated with parents and community leaders, and arranged for in-service education of the staff when such training was required.[9]

Teachers were forever *de-skilled* by this process, making it difficult to gain recognition and respect from others and to attract and retain the most able

THE GREAT AMERICAN EDUCATION MACHINE.

intellectuals for their profession. Undoubtedly this system contributed greatly to the low status of teacher education in colleges and universities.

This description is, of course, a caricature of American schools, at least in recent years. However exaggerated it may be, there remains enough validity to the model to make it recognizable. Women still outnumber men in K-12 teaching staff; they continue to lack control of what they can teach, despite the fact that all have bachelor's degrees and most have master's degrees. Most administrators remain men, although the proportion of women moving into school administration ranks has been growing steadily. Teacher unions have been mainly interested in protecting job security for teachers and increasing their salaries and fringe benefits, yet they have been willing to accept the division of labor between teachers and administrators.

External regulation also has grown. In some cases the state departments of education or state legislatures have even decreed the number of minutes to be spent on each subject in the primary grades. The frequency of tests for students has increased, as have controls on teachers. The system we have today is a logical extension of what was put into place early in the century; it is a highly centralized, bureaucratized system with little flexibility for teachers, coupled with extensive regulations by federal and state governments.

There is another aspect of our schools that should be mentioned. As noted earlier, formal education was once restricted to children of wealthy families and was intended to prepare youth for college. The schools that were formed in the late nineteenth and early twentieth century were designed to be comprehensive schools, open to children of all social classes. The school was to provide experience in democracy where all levels of society came together and learned to work with one another. This was part of what made American education distinctive.[10]

In order to accommodate students with different talents and career ambitions, it was necessary to provide different curriculum tracks, especially during the high school grades. Thus, some students follow a college prep track, others a vocational education track, and still others a general track. In many cases the subjects taken by students are different: College prep students study Latin or a modern foreign language, calculus, and physics; vocational students take shop courses; general education students enroll in typing. In other cases, the courses are the same but offered at different levels of difficulty. For example, everyone may take algebra but one class is for *boneheads,* the other for those expecting to study math in the future. The result is that it is possible to attend the same high school and receive a very

different kind of education. Students in an academic track may be asked to work hard under demanding teachers whereas other students are permitted to coast or are even ignored because it is assumed that either they are incapable of doing higher quality work or will not need a more demanding curriculum, given the jobs they will likely perform following graduation.

This system seemed to work satisfactorily for many years, but its weaknesses have become apparent. More students now wish to attend college, and colleges are eager to have them. To the degree that such students have taken a less demanding high school course of study, they are either unlikely to succeed as college undergraduates or the colleges must lower their standards in order to retain them. Schools are less able to serve the needs of vocational students; vocational agriculture, auto shop, woodworking, etc.—once staples of the vocational curriculum—are less attractive and/or useful in the preparation for a career. The kinds of technical skills industry needs cannot be taught easily in most schools, because schools lack the computers and sophisticated tools found in industry. Furthermore, as approximately 80 percent of new jobs are to be found in the service sector of the economy, the skills that students require are not particularly the vocational skills schools have traditionally emphasized. Skills in communication, problem solving, decision making, and team building are more important today than in the past. These are skills all students should acquire in school, not only those who may go to college.

The main problem with American schools today is not that students are lazy and teachers are poorly trained; it is that a system designed to fit needs of the past no longer fits current needs. We require a different kind of school, one that focuses not on mass production, but one providing each child with the best education possible.

Top-Down Reform

The reformers in the top-down (TD) camp are largely people who have reached conclusions about what needs to be done to reform schools and who wish to put plans into play that will lead to the desired results. One is tempted to call this a national reform effort because most of the reformers do take a national perspective, but certain state reforms operate in a top-down fashion as well. The important distinction is that following one or more studies of what is wrong with schools and one or more commission reports with recommended solutions, machinery is set in motion to bring everyone into compliance with the new thinking.

This reform group is dominated by business and political leaders. People who make their living as educators can also be found in this camp, mainly as allies of business and industry. While there are subtle differences between Democrats and Republicans, between business and government, and within the business community, the differences are of minor consequence.

The top-down group contains such individuals and groups as the president of the United States, the National Governors' Association, the Business Roundtable, the U.S. Chamber of Commerce, the National Alliance for Business, and the heads of many individual firms: the governing class in the United States. This approach has the support of most of the American corporate and charitable foundations that support educational reform. It is not an exaggeration to refer to this as the *establishment reform group.*

TD reformers see schools as agents of society. Schools can be ordered to move in one direction or another according to what leaders in American society believe that society needs. School reform proposals are typically justified for the gains they will produce for society as a whole, rather than for what they will achieve for children and their teachers.

When education writers describe the policies of educational reform since 1983, they are largely discussing TD activities. The first wave of reform, extending from approximately 1983 to 1989, was one of rules and regulations. It was based upon the assumption that more could be squeezed from schools if more were demanded of students and teachers. This assumption led to new rules and regulations aimed at increasing high school graduation standards, extending the school day and school year, imposing tests at each grade level, mandating the time to be spent on each topic, and finding ways to recognize and reward the best teachers through career ladders and merit pay while attempting to weed out weak teacher candidates by requiring state examinations prior to the award of license. Business and government leaders worked as a team. Business provided incentives to schools, loaned executives to help draw up reform plans, and supported awards to teachers and successful schools; government assumed responsibility for passing laws and regulations that placed further controls on what schools could or could not do.

By 1989 it was clear that this reform scheme was largely a bust, although I do not recall any high officials publicly declaring: "I'm sorry; we were wrong; we wasted time, energy, and money; we shall have to start over." Students were staying in school longer, taking more tests and enduring more academic courses, but such indicators as SAT scores and better performance on international examinations had changed little, if at all.

The conclusion reached was not that the reforms had been unwise; only that they had been insufficient. Obviously schools were too sick to be cured by simply tightening up standards. More radical surgery would be required.

In 1989 two significant events occurred. President George Bush called the governors together for a summit meeting on education, held on the campus of the University of Virginia in Charlottesville in September, 1989. The purpose of the conference was to gain agreement among federal and state political leaders to a set of goals that could be pursued collectively by all. The result was six goals approved jointly by the president and the governors. These were:

1. By the year 2000, all children in America will start school ready to learn;

2. By the year 2000, the high school graduation rate will increase to at least 90 percent;

3. By the year 2000, American students will leave grades four, eight, and twelve having demonstrated competency in challenging subject matter including English, mathematics, science, history, and geography, and every school in America will ensure that all students learn to use their minds well, so they may be prepared for responsible citizenship, further learning, and productive employment in our modern economy;

4. By the year 2000, U.S. students will be first in the world in mathematics and science achievement;

5. By the year 2000, every adult American will be literate and will possess the knowledge and skills necessary to compete in a global economy and exercise the rights and responsibilities of citizenship;

6. By the year 2000, every school in America will be free of drugs and violence and will offer a disciplined environment conducive to learning.[11]

The rhetorical style in which these goals were stated are totally out of character with traditional ways Americans have thought about the relationship of government and schooling. It is very typical of business planning; it is also typical of authoritarian governments, ones that set five-year plans and mobilize their subjects behind such plans.

The year 1989 was significant for another reason. President Bush announced his plan to promote "break the mold schools." This would be done in two ways: Industry would form a private organization, the New American Schools Development Corporation (NASDC), which would be responsible for raising funds and supporting the development of a handful of model schools that could be emulated by all other schools across the nation. Next, Congress would be asked to appropriate sufficient funds to establish one "break the mold school" in every Congressional district, plus two additional in each state, for a total of 535 schools. NASDC was greeted less than enthusiastically by the business community but was ultimately able to raise sufficient funds to host a design competition and to award eleven design grants to groups who agreed to develop model schools. Congress was even less receptive to the idea of 535 "break-the-mold schools." That portion of the Bush plan was never legislated.

In 1991 the National Center on Education and the Economy joined with the Learning Research and Development Center at the University of Pittsburgh to design a national examination system. Their work, called the New Standards Project, began a process to set goals and standards for each grade level and subject area, leading to approved tests for all students. In 1994 Congress created the National Education Standards and Improvement Council, whose job is to endorse national and state standards meeting its approval. In the same year, reports were being completed by historians, geographers, mathematicians, and others regarding what the national standards should be in their area of specialization. In the summer of 1994 the U.S. Department of Education announced a competition to provide funds for organizations willing to work with states and local schools to bring state and local curriculum standards into alignment with the national standards.

Work is also underway at creating national performance examinations for teachers. In 1986 the Carnegie Forum on Teaching as a Profession issued a report, *A Nation Prepared: Teachers for the 21st Century*, calling for a National Board for Professional Teaching Standards. The following year the board was established with initial funding from the Carnegie Corporation. The intention of this board is to produce a set of examinations that will measure a teacher's performance. Presumably the criteria will be set so that only good teachers can pass and be judged *board certified*. The board's supporters believe that schools will prefer to hire *board certified* teachers, and that this process will raise the standards and the prestige of the teaching profession, and teachers who have passed the examinations will earn higher salaries. In January 1995 the board announced the names of 81 middle school teachers from 23 states who became the first American school teachers to earn national certification.

While some of these processes have advanced independently from each other, there are undeniable linkages across the various initiatives. In some cases the same foundations are the primary funders; there is also cross-fertilization of operating and advisory boards. The same individuals appear as directors or advisors across the projects.

Despite all protests to the contrary, this is a massive effort to shape the future of American education from a national, not necessarily a federal, perspective. It is based on the assumption that local officials do not have sufficient knowledge to plan the future of their schools. Those with a national (perhaps even international) perspective know best. Those with these insights include national foundations, the federal government, national professional organizations, and global business firms. Even a decade ago such a move to centralize education would have been unthinkable. Today it is proceeding rapidly with little or no resistance from local officials and with the enthusiastic support of state governors.

Marc S. Tucker and the National Center on Education and the Economy

Marc S. Tucker and his National Center on Education and the Economy, based in Rochester, New York, are the most important and the most powerful sources of energy and ideas for the national reform of American education. What Tucker and his organization have accomplished in less than a decade is extraordinary. In 1985 Tucker, who formerly worked as associate director for Education Policy and Organization at the National Institute of

Education within the U. S. Department of Education, was asked by the Carnegie Corporation to direct its newly established Carnegie Forum on Education and the Economy. In 1986 the forum issued a report, *A Nation Prepared: Teachers for the 21st Century,* with Tucker as the principal author. This led to the establishment of the National Board for Professional Teaching Standards, which Tucker headed briefly. In 1987 Tucker was invited to Rochester to give advice on the restructuring of Rochester schools. This led to a decision to reorganize the forum into the National Center on Education and the Economy, and to place its headquarters in Rochester, where with state support it could help the Rochester schools while becoming a force for reform in the state of New York and the nation as a whole.

In 1989 the center established the Commission on the Skills of the American Work Force, which in 1990 published a report called *America's Choice: high skills or low wages!*[12] This report drew the public's attention to the apparent gap between the skills of American workers when compared to workers in our industrial competitor nations, in particular Germany and Japan. The report, as suggested by the title, argued that unless the United States dramatically changes and improves its education and system of training, the U.S. worker will suffer a continuing decline in his standard of living. The report recommended that "A new educational standard should be set for all students to be met by age 16. This standard should be established nationally and benchmarked to the highest in the world." Students who had achieved a "national standard of excellence" would be awarded a Certificate of Initial Mastery (CIM). Following receipt of CIM, students would be allowed to pursue work, enter a college preparatory program, or study for a Technical and Professional Certificate. Students who failed to achieve a CIM, even after repeated attempts, would not be permitted to go to work until age 18. The CIM concept is a topic of discussion within many state departments of education across the nation.

Also in 1989 the center found the National Alliance for Restructuring Education. It began with four state education systems and five large urban districts. In 1995 the alliance partners taught nearly five million students in over 9000 schools. In July 1992 the alliance was selected as one of 11 "select design teams" by NASDC. This award expanded Tucker's focus from workforce education to the total restructuring of American schools. The award was renewed by NASDC in 1993 for two additional years of funding.

In 1991 the National Center joined with the Learning Research and Development Center at the University of Pittsburgh to establish the New Standards Project, a national effort to set world-class standards for student achievement and to develop a student performance assessment system to measure student progress against those standards. Pew Charitable Trust and the John D. and Catherine T. MacArthur Foundation provided over $8 million to fund this work. A group of 17 states and six school districts, involving more than half of the nation's students, are participating in the development and pilot testing of the new standards and examinations.

In 1993 the center advised the Clinton administration in helping frame federal education and training legislation, such as the *Goals 2000: Educate America Act* and the *School to Work Transition Opportunities Act*. One part of this legislation provided for the establishment of the National Education Standards and Improvement Council that will decide which state and national standards should be endorsed. In less than a decade, Tucker and the National Center for Education and the Economy have become a powerful force for setting the national education agenda.

Making Education More Like Business. In 1992 Tucker and Ray Marshall, former Secretary of Labor under President Jimmy Carter and co-chair of the Commission on the Skills of the American Work Force, published *Thinking for a Living: Education and the Wealth of Nations.*[13] This book eloquently sets forth a point of view regarding the problems confronting the American economy and offers recommendations for changing the American educational system in order to overcome these problems. This work is the best single source I have found for understanding the perspective of those who wish to take a TD approach to school reform in order to solve America's economic problems.

Marshall and Tucker coined the term "human-resource capitalism." It assumes that the key to future wealth lies in having access to an adequate supply of highly skilled labor, a business strategy that emphasizes quality and productivity, and a way of organizing work that takes advantage of these concepts.

The authors describe in detail the problems that American businesses face in global competition; they argue that deficiencies in the skills of the American workforce are the single greatest problem to be overcome. They acknowledge that American schools have served the economy well for most of the twentieth century, but they argue that the formula that once resulted in American economic power and a high standard of living for most Americans will not work any longer. American business must change if it is to be competitive; as it changes, it must have access to larger numbers of skilled workers than before. It will find them either in the United States or in nations that provide highly skilled workers willing to work for low wages.

The authors seek to do what Franklin Bobbitt and others did for American education at the turn of the century: align schools with the needs of business. American educators may dislike having business interests and the economy serve as the driving force for school reform, but there is no doubt that top-down reforms are being advanced on the basis of what will be good for the economy as a whole.

American business has also acquired useful knowledge during the process of *reengineering*. This knowledge can be applied to restructuring education. If business can teach schools a thing or two, what are some of the lessons that schools can learn from business?

1. *Move decision making to the lowest possible level and eliminate middle layers of management.* This results in better decisions and makes the company leaner and more productive. In education, this calls for site-based decision making and the elimination of central office bureaucrats.

2. *Business must give customers what they want.* This has led in business to customization within mass production. In education this means finding a way to give parents and students greater choice and more control over their education.

3. *Quality is preeminent and a given.* Customers continue to look for the best price for whatever they purchase, but they assume high quality at whatever price they must pay. In schools, this means accepting the idea that all students can learn; it is the job of the school to make certain that all students have access to demanding instruction.

4. *It is expensive to repair flaws after they have been built into the product.* The answer is to get it right the first time and keep it right rather than try to repair the problem later. In education, this means not passing students who have failed to learn what they need to know. Advancing students to the next grade level before they have mastered the subjects of the preceding one merely presents additional problems to the teachers who will meet them later. It is less expensive to give students the extra time and attention they require when the problem appears than to graduate them with weaknesses or try to fix the problem at upper grades or later, when they go to college.

5. *In order to know when one has high quality, one must "benchmark" the processes as well as the final products of a firm's major competitors.* Thus, the Ford Motor Company attempts to produce cars of a higher quality more efficiently than does General Motors, Honda, or Toyota. In education, this means establishing national goals and standards and comparing the performance of our students to those attending schools in Germany and Japan.

6. *While decision making should be driven down to the lowest possible level of activity, those who make decisions should be fully accountable for their actions by examining their profitability.* In education, schools must be held accountable by some form of acceptable system of national or state approved achievement tests. Good teachers should be paid more and given greater responsibility than weaker teachers.

7. *The quality of the labor force will determine the success or failure of the firm in global markets.* The workforce requires top-flight knowledge and skills and the willingness to continue to learn as conditions change. In education, this means improving the quality of initial teacher education and making certain that further professional education serves the needs of the teacher workforce.

For the most part, Tucker's ideas are good ones; they could contribute to better school practices. There are some important differences, however, between business and education that are often overlooked by fervent reformers. For example, manufacturers assume that the production of high quality products begins with superior raw materials. No manufacturer would be ready to compare his products with others if he is denied good raw material. American schools do not have the luxury of admitting only those students who are able to learn easily; they must accept everyone who arrives at their door. Indeed, the same political leaders demanding higher quality results are the same ones insisting schools accept and retain students who would likely have not attended school thirty years ago.

Finally, TD reformers appear to want to strike a bargain with schools. They say:

1. *If* the schools will educate all children to a level beyond that which, in the past, it prepared only the academic elite; and

2. *If* the schools are willing to be accountable for the results of their effort by various kinds of national examinations;

3. *Then,* government will deregulate schools, leaving decisions in the hands of teachers, principals, and parents regarding how instruction is to be designed to produce the required levels of excellence; and

4. As positive results are forthcoming, schools will be rewarded by additional funds to further enhance their work.

The TD justification for school reform is that it is necessary in order to have a strong economy. To have a strong education system, it will be necessary to change the way schools operate today. TD reformers believe that if schools do not change, America will become weaker. Because the president, the governors, business leaders, national foundations, and some educational reformers understand what is needed more than teachers, administrators, and local school boards, it is the responsibility of government and business leaders to decide what school reforms are needed and how reform will be accomplished.

Bottom-Up Reform

Bottom-up (BU) reformers stand for people and organizations that are suspicious of reform proposals that treat schools as if they were all the same. As a group, they are people who have studied schools for years and tend to be impressed by the differences among schools and the ways each school must respond to its own cultural setting. While their recommendations sometimes overlap with the TD group, they did not reach their conclusions by the same process nor do they justify their proposals by referring to some overarching cause, such as strengthening the American economy, or supporting national defense. They tend to ground their arguments on the basis of what they think would be best for students and teachers.

Many BU reformers could be mentioned. Among the best known are James Comer, who heads the School Development Program for Yale University's Child Study Center; John Goodlad, who directs the Center for Educational Renewal at the University of Washington; Henry Levin, director of the Accelerated Schools Project at Stanford; Ted Sizer, director of the Coalition for Essential Schools at Brown University; and Robert Slavin, director of the Elementary School Program, Center for Research on Effective Schooling for Disadvantaged Students at Johns Hopkins University. Notice that all are based at universities. Each has been engaged in the study of schools for a decade or longer; each has reached conclusions about what needs to be done; each has followers; each has been funded substantially by federal and private grants; each has a large organization behind him; each wields substantial influence over the education community and is respected by public policy makers. As contrasted to the hundreds of other educators who offer advice in articles and books regarding what should be done to reform education, these individuals have tested their ideas over an extended period of time in schools. If there can be such a thing, they are the *education establishment* among education reformers.

Each of the reformers cited above has his own ideas about what needs to be done, yet they tend to share the same bias. Unlike the TD people, they doubt that much can or will be accomplished by such devices as national plans, schemes, goals, standards, tests, and regulations. From their experience, they are impressed by how different schools are and how difficult it is to offer prescriptions that fit all circumstances. They also see the school—even the individual classroom—as the front line of reform. Whatever may be announced nationally will be of little consequence unless it squares with what an individual teacher believes is possible to do with her own students. While they do not shrink from articulating principles that they believe to be appropriate in all schools, they are enormously patient in allowing each school, even each teacher, to decide how those principles fit his/her own circumstance. They believe school reform will not be accomplished by federal mandates; it will be done the hard way: one school at a time.

Theodore R. (Ted) Sizer and the Coalition of Essential Schools

At the time of this writing Ted Sizer and his Coalition of Essential Schools are the most influential of the BU group. Sizer has served in various roles. He was a history teacher, a headmaster of Phillips Andover Academy, dean of the Graduate School of Education at Harvard University, and most recently, professor of Education at Brown University. In 1984 he published a highly acclaimed book, *Horace's Compromise: The Dilemma of the American High School,*[14] a report of a five-year study of American high schools, sponsored by the National Association of Secondary School Principals and the Commission on Educational Issues of the National Association of Independent Schools. The book sought to explain how the nature of students, the character of the high school program, teaching conditions, and the structure of schooling work together to produce less than optimum results. Horace's "compromise" consists of the various accommodations that a fictionalized teacher named Horace Smith makes to the forces that operate upon him.

Following the publication of the book, Sizer discovered a group of teachers and schools that were eager to test his ideas, and foundations that were willing to support his approach. In 1984 he founded the Coalition of Essential Schools, a high school/university partnership that attempts to redesign schools for better student learning and achievement. From 12 charter schools in four states, the coalition has grown to include more than 180 member schools in more than 30 states. Nearly 600 additional schools are either exploring coalition school principles or are preparing to become active members of the coalition.

By 1988 it was apparent that many of the principles that schools in the coalition wished to pursue conflicted with rules and regulations in force in the 50 states. As a result Sizer struck an alliance with the Education Commission of the States, a policy and research center created in 1965. The result is a project called "Re: Learning," which attempts to identify school system policies and management practices that interfere with learning while pursuing changes in instructional practice. In a sense, "Re: Learning" is an attempt to wed top-down and bottom-up approaches.

In 1992 Sizer published a second book, *Horace's School: Redesigning the American High School.*[15] This book places the imaginary Horace Smith in charge of a committee to recommend a series of changes for the fictitious Franklin High School. Sizer uses the imaginary debates among the committee members to highlight how difficult it is to bring about change in schools.

From the two books, it is possible to derive some of Sizer's assumptions about schools. Perhaps the most important is that schools are not the same: Students are different, communities are different, teachers are different; it is foolish to treat them as if they all were the same. Second, there is too much mistrust: Teachers mistrust students; students mistrust teachers; administrators mistrust teachers and vice versa; public officials distrust educators; school officials mistrust the communities they serve; and the general public frequently distrusts those in charge of schools. Little will be accomplished until trust is restored across all levels of schooling and society. Third, adults pamper American students; teachers demand too little of students; students are given too little responsibility; in turn, students demand too little of their teachers, especially in the high school grades. Young people on the verge of becoming fully adult in the eyes of society are treated as young children incapable of assuming responsibility for their own learning. The result is that schooling in general, and high school in particular, is too easy and fails to challenge most students. Fourth, while learning may be natural and can be fun, serious learning is also hard; nevertheless, children can and will learn if they are able to learn what is asked of them and if they believe what they are learning will prove to be of some value to them. Good teaching is also hard work and is generally unappreciated by those outside of the profession. Fifth, we make instruction more difficult than it needs to be by attempting to cover too much material too rapidly, leading to superficial teaching and learning. In instruction, as in some other aspects of life, less is more. The problem of superficiality is further exaggerated by the type of examinations given to students. Such exams reward rote memorization and short-term recall of information rather than deep understanding. And sixth, there are limits to what the state can legitimately demand of students. The public may expect that all students should acquire levels of literacy and numeracy sufficient to operate in society and that they understand the rights and responsibilities of citizenship, but the state has no right to push students toward college or particular careers. The level of education required of a student and what he does with his education should be for him to decide. It is improper in a democracy for the state to design schools so that students are trained to serve a national cause. It should be obvious that BU reformers do not agree with many of the assumptions and recommendations of TD reformers.

From these assumptions, Sizer has articulated nine common principles that characterize "essential schools." How these principles are actually applied vary greatly from school to school, but all of the schools agree to abide by these principles.[16]

1. The school should focus on helping adolescents learn to use their minds well. Schools should not attempt to be "comprehensive" if such a claim is made at the expense of the school's central intellectual purpose.

2. The school's goals should be simple: Each student should master a number of essential skills and be competent in certain areas of knowledge. Although these skills and areas will, to varying degrees, reflect the traditional academic disciplines, the program's design should be shaped by the intellectual and imaginative powers and competencies that students need, rather than by conventional "subjects." The aphorism "less is more" should dominate: Curricular decisions are to be directed toward students' attempt to gain mastery rather than by the teachers' effort to cover content.

3. The school's goals should apply to all students, but the means to these goals will vary as these students themselves vary. School practice should be tailor-made to meet the needs of every group of adolescents.

4. Teaching and learning should be personalized to the maximum feasible extent. No teacher should have direct responsibility for more than eighty students; decisions about the course of study, the use of students' and teachers' time, and the choice of teaching materials and specific pedagogies must be placed in the hands of the principal and staff.

5. The governing metaphor of the school should be student as worker, rather than the more familiar metaphor of teacher as deliverer of instructional services. Accordingly, a prominent pedagogy will be coaching, to provoke students to learn and thus to teach themselves.

6. Students embarking on secondary school studies are those who show competence in language and elementary mathematics. Students of traditional high school age who do not yet have appropriate levels of competence to start secondary school studies will be provided with intensive remedial work so that they can quickly meet those standards. The diploma should be awarded on a successful final demonstration of mastery for graduation—an Exhibition. This Exhibition by the student of his or her grasp of the central skills and knowledge of the school's program may be jointly administered by the faculty and higher authorities. Because the diploma is awarded when earned, the school's program proceeds with no strict age grading and with no system of credits earned by time spent in class. The emphasis is on the students' demonstration that they can do important things.

7. The tone of the school should explicitly and self-consciously stress the values of unanxious expectation ('I won't threaten you, but I expect much of you'), of trust (unless it is abused), and of decency (the values of fairness, generosity, and tolerance). Incentives appropriate to the school's students and teachers should be emphasized, and parents should be treated as essential collaborators.

8. The principal and teachers should perceive of themselves first as generalists (teachers and scholars in general education) and next as specialists (experts in a particular discipline). Staff should expect multiple obligations (teacher-counselor-manager) and a sense of commitment to the entire school.

9. Administrative and budget targets should include substantial time for collective planning by teachers, competitive salaries for staff, and an ultimate per-pupil cost not more than 10 percent higher than that at traditional schools. Administrative plans may have to show the phased reduction or elimination of some services now provided for students in many traditional comprehensive secondary schools.

What can be said of Sizer's ideas? He imagines a reform that must occur school by school, with no school being identical to the other. Further, he perceives the focus of the problem and the solution to lie in individual classrooms and the interaction between teachers and students. He believes too little is asked of students and too much of teachers. He would have public schools become more like the best private schools, where teachers have the time to truly know their students, and where each school acquires a personality of its own, reflecting the community it serves.

Sizer's schools are not easily mobilized behind a national cause, nor will it be easy to hold them accountable for national goals, standards, and examinations. Sizer's goal is to make schools places where thinking is valued and where students learn to enjoy using their minds. Everything else is incidental.

Sizer's influence is comparable to that of Marc Tucker's. Like Tucker, Sizer and the Coalition of Essential Schools, in partnership with others, has received funding from NASDC to create model schools to be emulated by others. Even more important is that in October 1993, Brown University announced that it would establish The Annenberg Institute for School Reform and that Ted Sizer would serve as its founding director. With major support from the Walter H. Annenberg Foundation, the institute is expected to become a gathering place for debate and investigation for all of those concerned with the quality of schooling. The institute has based its activities on four principles: 1) All children must learn and learn well; 2) each child in school must be well known and taught in ways appropriate to his or her development; 3) rigorous intellectual performance is expected of every student and is exhibited by means of public demonstration of the student's real work through exhibitions, portfolios, and projects; and 4) schools should reinforce democracy at the community level, balancing opportunities inherent in the diversity of American cultures with the need for a universally thoughtful and intellectually flexible citizenry. Special attention must be given to the views of parents and students within each school community.

Thus, those who favor BU approaches to reform now have a well-funded institute to which they can look for inspiration and leadership. Given the institute's likely influence on future awards by Annenberg and other foundations, Sizer is well-placed to provide leadership for school reform for many years.

Students, Teachers and School Administrators

If it is difficult to represent the separate views of individual reformers; it is even more difficult to represent the separate views of 41 million students, 2,450,000 teachers, and 200,000 administrators. Yet to ignore the views of those who are the objects of school reform is even more foolish.

I do not mean to imply that those who work within schools have been ignored; they have not. Representatives of students, teachers, and administrators have been invited to serve on and to testify before national commissions, and educational reformers such as John Goodlad and Ted Sizer have spent years in the schools, observing school practices and talking to students, teachers, and administrators. Nevertheless, the views of those inside the schools tend to get merged with and used as evidence for what people outside of schools believe should happen.

Rather than provide my own interpretations of what students, teachers, and administrators believe, I have chosen to rely on a recent study of four California schools. The study, *Voices from the Inside: A Report on Schooling from Inside the Classrooms* by Mary Poplin and Joseph Weeres, was published in November 1992.[17] The study was conducted over an 18-month period with extensive observations in four representative urban/suburban public schools (two elementary schools, one middle school, and one high school) and sustained conversations with students, staff, and parents. The investigators chose to let the school participants speak for themselves regarding what they liked and did not like about their schools. And while there may be a bias toward multicultural issues because of the location of the schools and the nature of the student bodies, the investigators believe that the issues they discovered are likely to correspond with issues in other schools.

One major conclusion the investigators reached was that many of the school *problems* emphasized by education reformers (e.g., low test scores, high dropout rates, low morale among teachers) were in fact *indicators* of more deep-seated problems. If this is true, then many reforms are misdirected. It is as if we treated fatigue and a higher than average temperature as the problem rather than attempting to solve the underlying disease that created the symptoms.

Poplin and Weeres classified their data according to seven major issues: relationships; race, culture, and class; values; teaching and learning; safety; physical environment; and despair, hope, and the process of change. I shall touch upon each briefly.

Relationships. Many students, parents, and staff felt that relationships among people in the four schools were not what they should be. Students were overjoyed when they were able to know a teacher well, and teachers commented that their greatest pleasure came from knowing a student and being able to help him or her. Teachers were sad because there was too little time and too many students to do what would be required to know their students well. Teachers also complained that they scarcely knew their colleagues and had little time to discuss issues relating to curriculum and instruction with them.

Race, Culture, and Class. Students experienced racism and sexism from fellow students and sometimes from their teachers and school staff. Many students were bilingual; most teachers were not. Students were eager to learn about their own cultures and that of their classmates, but there was little time to do so. Students often distrusted their textbooks because they believed them to be biased against their race, culture, or social class.

Values. To the surprise of the investigators, and despite the wide cultural differences, there were few differences among students and staff with regard to fundamental values. They all cherished a sound education, honesty, integrity, justice, truth, courage, and meaningful hard work. However, the school afforded little opportunity to discuss values, and the students longed for many more opportunities for value discussions than they were offered.

Teaching and Learning. School seemed fun and exciting for elementary students, but by middle school and high school, students and teachers found school boring much of the time. Students saw little meaning in what they were asked to study; many teachers saw little purpose in their subjects either, yet the topics were mandated and had to be covered. From the teachers' point of view, achievement tests were very influential in deciding what should be taught.

Students longed for more activities and more opportunities to share ideas with their classmates. Teachers said they knew that they could teach better than they did, but they had little time for adequate preparation.

Safety. Very few participants felt the schools were as safe as they should be. This was especially true in middle school and high school, where students feared physical violence as a result of drugs and gang activity. Some of the fear students had of other students seemed to be the result of the lack of knowledge of other races, cultures, and social classes.

The concern for safety squares exactly with the results of the 1994 PDK/Gallup Poll on education, in which 18 percent of those polled thought that "fighting/violence, gangs" was the number one problem confronting schools while an equal percentage believed lack of discipline to be the biggest problem. These two issues were judged to be far more important than such issues as poor curriculum/low curriculum standards (3%) or difficulty in getting good teachers (3%).

Physical Environment. Except for one new school, the remaining three schools showed deterioration and lack of adequate maintenance. Classes were crowded; in some cases there were not even enough desks for all of the students unless some students were absent. Equipment and instructional materials were in short supply. Most teachers had no funds for classroom expenditures. The average teacher in the four schools spent $500 annually of her own money on student materials; this ranged from teachers who spent nothing for this purpose to teachers who spent as much as $2,000 during a school year to compensate for lack of funding by the school system.

These findings are consistent with a study conducted by the General Accounting Office in 1994 and published in February 1995. According to the GAO report, one-third of the nation's 80,000 public schools are in such poor repair that they provide unsafe or unsuitable conditions for the 14 million students who must attend them. The cost of correcting conditions in American schools was estimated to be $112 billion.[18]

Despair, Hope, and Change. The investigators found that there were moments of great joy in the schools, but overall there was a sense of despair. Students were quite conscious of the problems that existed in the society at large and worried about their ability to meet them. Teachers and administrators were frustrated by limits on their ability to respond to their students' needs. Most felt a need for substantial change in school, but there was doubt that meaningful change could be accomplished within the constraints imposed on schools.

If the attitudes of teachers, administrators, students, and parents reported in the Claremont study are typical of the attitudes of such groups nationally, then many school reforms may exacerbate problems rather than correct them. We may choose to hold schools accountable for national standards and tests, but what does this mean when schools are unable to provide a desk for each student and teachers must buy instructional materials with their own salaries?

Conclusion

School reform is underway; it is too soon to judge if it will be successful. The publicly stated rationale for school reform—to make schools as good as they once were or as good as schools in competitor nations or to use schools to rescue the American economy—is suspect. It is not that schools should avoid change, but why schools need to change, in what direction they should change, and how they can best change are not topics on which there is universal agreement. TD reformers have one set of opinions as do BU reformers, as do teachers, administrators and students.

The desires of students, parents, and administrators, such as those described above in the Poplin and Weeres' study, should be the easiest to resolve, if we are willing to invest more money. Schools would not have to change their essential structure to please them. In contrast, TD reformers will not be happy until all schools have changed in particular ways; BU reformers want schools to change markedly, but they are willing to leave the details to individual schools.

Role of Technology

Technology is not featured in the reform plans of any of these groups. The educators and parents studied by Poplin and Weeres might desire technology if they thought it were possible, but when they lack adequate desks, when teachers must supplement the purchase of school supplies from their own salaries, and when school buildings are poorly maintained, it must be hard to imagine a time when students and teachers would have their own computers.

Marc Tucker has, at other times, been an advocate of technology and sees an important role for technology in the school reform effort, including using technology for building portfolios and for communication among schools. Ted Sizer, who had exhibited no particular interest in technology in the past, has been exploring ways technology can be used to support school redesign principles. IBM is assisting the coalition's efforts to use digital databases for storing student portfolios; an electronic mail network connects reformers with many of the coalition schools; teachers are encouraged to use presentation software and simulations in their classrooms; and staff are producing live video teleconferences originating from coalition schools that demonstrate model practices to schools receiving the programs.

These and other efforts indicate ways that reformers are attempting to use technology to implement their ideas by fostering improved communication, teaching, and testing. However, none of these reformers envision the impact technology could have on the total operation, structure, and culture of the school.

Probable Success of School Reform

Which approach to school reform is most likely to succeed—the national, top-down approach or the bottom-up, one-school-at-a-time strategy? Is it possible to impose one broad solution on widely diverse communities? Can we wait until American education is reformed one classroom or one school at a time? No one can answer these questions confidently.

We should not overlook one issue. While schools serve students, they also serve teachers. Unless teachers are happy in their work and are inspired by their responsibilities, very little will happen to change the way schools conduct their business, regardless of all of the reform documents and public appeals by American business and governmental leaders. Successful instruction depends upon personal interaction between a teacher and a student. Unless reform takes place at this level, talk of school reform is just talk.

Chapter 3

TEACHING AND LEARNING IN THE INFORMATION AGE

Telling is not teaching; listening is not learning. Anonymous

All of the demands for school reform and all of the proposals for changing schools will be for naught unless there are dramatic gains in student learning. The main reason we fund public schools is the belief that schools provide a cost-effective means for enabling American youngsters to learn what they need to know. If the public were to conclude that other means can provide instruction as well or better in a more cost-effective manner, the public schools would likely lose their mandate as well as control of public funds for the schooling of most young Americans.

Whatever success schools may have enjoyed in the past and however much unjustified criticism they may receive today, none of this matters. The fact is that many public officials, business leaders, and educators believe that schools can do better. They must do better!

The primary place where school learning occurs is in individual classrooms. Whether classroom learning takes place or not depends mainly upon the interactions of individual students with their teachers. It is true that students learn from each other, and that the school culture and the community also function as teachers. Yet the most important key to learning is the relationship between the student and his teacher. If learning is to become better, teachers must become more effective.

No one should doubt my own commitment to public education or my personal regard for many schools and individual teachers; some of the best teachers I have known were once colleagues; others have taught my own children. At the same time, I know—and most teachers know—that public schools can do better. The opportunities for students to learn are not as rich as they could be. We often do not teach as well as we know how. And students are not learning anywhere near their capabilities.

Teaching well and helping children and youth learn to the level of their ability is more important today than in the past. In the Information Age, the ability to learn quickly is the most important asset an individual can acquire. In the past a strong back and a willingness to work hard might have been enough, but these traits are no longer sufficient. While learning is a natural act and people can learn much from direct experience, teachers can help students become self-conscious learners: They can assist them in improving their learning skills, inspire them to acquire knowledge they might not otherwise encounter, and equip them with tools for abstract thought that will make their practical experience more meaningful. Schools are essential for the intellectual development of individuals; they are also vital to the development of the most important assets of a community. How can teaching and learning become more effective? What are the obstacles that stand in the way of progress?

Typical Classrooms Today

Over the past two decades, many observers have painted a dismal picture of a typical classroom and a typical school day, especially for middle school and high school age students. First of all, teachers seem to be doing most of the work, while many students appear to be only partially engaged with the instruction. It is not that teachers lecture constantly; indeed, teachers use class time largely to reinforce and to supplement what students were expected to have read in their textbooks or other materials supplied by their teachers. The teacher instructs in at least three ways: by explaining what the textbook presented so that the content will be understood by even the slowest in the class, by adding information related to the points made in the text, and by asking questions of students to ascertain whether they have understood what they have read. From time to time, an experienced teacher will cue her students by saying, "Now this is really important. You can expect it on the test."

Any typical classroom contains able and conscientious students who already understand what the teacher is explaining laboriously to slower students and who could easily answer all of the teacher's questions if the teacher allowed them to do so; the same classroom also has other students who either lack interest, are unprepared for the lesson, or do not have the necessary foundation for understanding the instruction. The result is usually a pedagogical compromise: The teacher will direct her instruction toward what she perceives to be the middle tier of students, recognizing that she is moving too slowly and boring the best students while denying the weakest pupils sufficient time and help to understand the content fully. This is the

"Starting school, Stanley, is just like going on a really long fact-finding tour."

standard predicament of group instruction. Unless the teacher is able to individualize instruction so that it fits the ability and interest level of each student or unless students can be grouped according to interest and ability level, compromise is inevitable. The current opposition of educators to "tracking" students and the requirement that children with various handicaps be "mainstreamed" or included in regular courses have made the instructional problem for teachers even greater.

A second common feature of typical classrooms is the assignment of routine work for students to perform during a portion of the class hour. This may take the form of published worksheets that accompany the textbook or they may be materials that the teacher created herself. In any case, students are expected to work diligently on tasks that may be another way to review the textbook content. In mathematics classes these exercises are likely to be further math problems; in English classes they may be grammar exercises; in history or geography classes they may be drills on who did what or where did things occur. In some cases, such work may be assigned as homework. More commonly, these tasks are completed within the class hour or they are not accomplished at all. Teachers can use this assignment time to give special attention to weaker students.

There are many other ways teachers can—and sometimes do—teach, including allowing students to work in groups, encouraging individual student investigations. However, guided recitation and written assignments for the class as a whole enhance teacher control over the class; and teacher control is fundamental. Those who have not taught children and youth are unlikely to appreciate the importance teachers assign to classroom control. It is not that most teachers fear their students; rather, they fear chaos. They know how easily young adolescents can be distracted and how difficult it is to focus their energy on learning some new information or skill; teachers therefore generally resist instructional practices that seem to undermine their control of what is permitted to take place in their classroom.

All of the teacher's work and student effort is focused on preparing for *the test.* Seldom is this the SAT test or even a state or national achievement test. It is the test given at the close of a unit of study, sometimes as frequently as every week, and more commonly every two or three weeks. The unit test determines whether students have learned and justifies why they have bothered to learn it. The test also sorts students along a grading curve. Because one of the important tasks of teachers is assigning grades, the test provides a defensible measure for giving one student an A, a second a B, a third a C, and so on.

As a result, from the students' point of view, the principal reason they study world history is to take tests on world history. The teacher may have quite different reasons for the study of world history, e.g., cultural enlightenment, to become a more knowledgeable reader; for her the test is mainly a device to reward effort and punish sloth. In either way, the test drives the system—but not for all students. Some students have given up. They have attended classes with the same students long enough to know who the A and B students are, and they know if they are a C student. They cannot imagine themselves getting an A, nor could their teachers. Thus, they do enough to get their usual C. Test results usually reassure the teacher because student scores typically approximate what she would have predicted. Only if a good student does poorly or if a poor student does very well is there cause for alarm.

The test has another effect. Once a student has taken the test, he has little or no further responsibility for the content covered. There might be a test at the end of the course, but the teacher will usually provide time to review for that test. Once a student has finished his study of the Roman Empire in the world history course, he is able to forget the Romans; he is unlikely to hear from them again.

Our schools may do a good job of cultivating short-term memory. Any who attended an American school, and who was successful in school, knows how to cram for a unit or semester test and then forget what was learned after there is no further use of the data. Those who want to add further testing to schooling by means of national exams should recognize that we already have test-driven schools, but students have developed their own ways of accommodating their demands. National tests will not likely have the impact on American students that they do in Europe, where tests are employed less frequently and students are expected to retain knowledge over a much longer period of time.

Attending class is seen as an individual activity within a group setting. The knowledge one acquires from instruction is an individual property. Each student must get all, some, or none of it for himself. Students are not permitted to help one another; that is cheating. Each student is expected to do the tasks by himself, with perhaps a little assistance from parents. It is less important that the student know it (whatever *it* is) than that the student acquire it on his own. It would complicate assessment if a student knew something after having learned it from a classmate. It seems to be better to work hard and fail than to work hard in partnership with another and succeed.

Another feature of classroom interactions between teachers and students are the bargains that are struck regarding how much work will be done and what will be counted as acceptable quality. The bargaining is never explicit, but experienced teachers and students intuitively know the process and rules.

The bargaining usually starts at the beginning of each academic year when the teacher announces the standards for the course: how many papers will be required, her policy on homework and deductions of credit on late papers, and so on. This is akin to a seller announcing he will take no less than $150,000 for his house, before the buyer states his highest offer. Day by day, students chip away at the standards. For example: "Can I use the same paper for your class that I have written for my world history class?" "I can't turn my paper in on Friday; I have been rehearsing for the school play all week and the performance is Friday." And so it goes. One reasonable excuse yields a concession to be followed by others. The teacher attempts to make the class as demanding as possible without becoming foolish or tyrannical. The students meanwhile negotiate the least amount of work possible, because little of it seems important to them anyway. The result is that if the teacher is reasonable and not too demanding, the students will be reasonable too by generally going along with the teacher and raising no problems. The teacher has no recourse but to bargain; if she stays with a high standard and students refuse to perform, the entire class might fail.

Of course, the standards are not the same for every class. If one is teaching an Advanced Placement (AP) class, it is assumed that students will do more work and higher quality work than will students in the general curriculum. If the AP students did not expect to do more, they should not have enrolled in an Advanced Placement class. Yet bargaining is not restricted to those students enrolled in the general and vocational tracks; the very brightest will also calculate the minimum effort they must make to get an A grade.

What is missing is an agreed-upon cultural norm that everyone does his or her best work all of the time. In schools such a norm is more likely to be found in athletics and some other extracurricular activities.

The peer group helps shape the school's norms. Within every high school, cliques are formed around different identities: the "jocks," the "preppies," the "greasers." There is usually a clique for the "brains" as well, but they are rarely the most popular, unless they also happen to be athletes or preppies. Other students see the academically high performers as the "Stakhanovites" of the school, making school harder for others, and not playing the game. Strangely enough, the brainy kids are not always the most popular with the teachers either. While for some teachers they provide an exquisite joy, others find such students upsetting precisely because they know more than other students and demand more than the teacher is able to give.

The final point to be made about school, at least secondary school, is how disjointed it is. Teachers seldom notice, because from their perspective, there is a steady flow to their instruction: One unit leads to another, one lesson builds upon the preceding one. But from the students' perspective a school day is very different. For example, take an imaginary high school sophomore named Bob. Here was his schedule for a typical day:

8:00   Bob arrived at school after a 35-minute bus ride.

8:20   World History: The lesson was on the "New Deal in Old Rome." The teacher explained that "new deal" referred to policies associated with President Franklin D. Roosevelt; the teacher described a few of Roosevelt's ideas in order to compare policies of the Gracchi brothers with Roosevelt's New Deal policies.

9:10   Physical Education: Because it was a warm day, the physical education class was held outside. The boys played soccer; the girls played softball on another field.

10:00 Home Room: This period provided a time for clubs to meet. Bob used it as a time to cram for his German exam. By agreement among teachers in this school, exams are given on designated days according to subject areas; the result is that there may be an exam in one of Bob's courses on every day of the week.

10:30 Geometry: The class had a test on the preceding day; this day was devoted to reviewing the test and helping students to understand their errors. Bob had scored well on the test; he used the time mainly to prepare for the German exam.

11:20 Biology: The lesson was on the function of the nervous system. The teacher led a recitation over the textbook assignment. The class had a few minutes to glance briefly at a few specimens displayed on tables at the back of the classroom. The biology teacher reminded students of the test on the nervous system scheduled for the next day. All the talk of nervous systems unnerved Bob.

12:10 Lunch: Bob rushed to the cafeteria, took five minutes to go through the cafeteria line and 10 minutes to gulp down his lunch. This allowed 15 minutes to visit briefly with friends, go to the toilet, and make it to English class.

12:40 English: The regular teacher was absent from class; the substitute teacher assigned a short story to be read during the class period in order that it could be discussed the following day. In effect, the students were given a free study period. Bob was delighted. He postponed reading the story until after school and continued to study for his German exam.

1:30 German: The test was on the conjugation of a select number of German verbs, applying them correctly in sentences. Bob had seen all of these sentences before in his German book. With a total of nearly two and one-half hours to study for the test, he knew them well. German is his hardest subject, but on this test he expects to receive a good grade.

2:20 Band practice: Bob plays a baritone horn. The director rehearsed some new music the band will perform at the mid-winter concert.

3:10 Classes were adjourned: Bob did not ride a bus home. He stayed behind for football practice. An older teammate who lives close to him dropped him off at his home around 5:30 when practice was over.

This was a fairly typical day for Bob. Some portions of the day were undemanding. Indeed, the lack of pressure in the geometry class and English class worked to Bob's advantage; it enabled him to prepare better for his German test. Students less conscientious than Bob would have had a fairly relaxed day. But what is striking is how much of the day is devoted to starting and stopping topics and how unrelated each period is to the other. This is the Industrial Age model of schooling in full bloom.

Why do we have such a system? Partly it is traditional. With the onset of school attendance laws, school became something one had to do. School is not unpleasant for most students, but one has no choice about whether to attend school or not. Therefore, a kind of game is made out of it, a game in which teachers either consciously or unconsciously participate. The fact that some states now wish to extend compulsory attendance from age 16 to age 18 is unlikely to have any impact on this game.

The kind of school we have fits roughly what schools were designed to be. They are intended to be places where naive learners gather to learn what they need to know from an expert teacher. What seems different today is that students seem less naive than in the past and less interested in what schools believe students should learn.

There are other factors that affect classroom learning. Students do not arrive at school without knowledge; all have learned a great deal from prior schooling as well as from sources outside of school. For example, we frequently complain about the number of hours American youngsters watch television; certainly, television can encourage passivity and provide a distraction from school work. But children and youth are also learning constantly from television and other media—much of it wrong, but learned in any case. For example, what have students learned of World War II by watching *Hogan's Heroes* or of the Korean War by watching *MASH?*

Teachers also often complain about the lack of support they receive from parents. It is not that parents have less interest in their children today, but the rise of divorce, single-parent families, and two working parents have put additional stress on families, distracting them from school activities. Today, parents generally have more education than did parents in the past; they own books on child psychology and have strong opinions about schooling, and are less likely to defer to teachers.

Albert Shanker, head of the American Federation of Teachers, believes that student apathy exists in part because there are few consequences for students doing poorly in school. Employers may require a high school diploma for employment, but they rarely ask to see a student transcript; and nearly every student who graduates from high school will find a college somewhere that will accept him. Making high school graduation count for more might lead students to take school more seriously.

Americans also seem fatalistic about learning. Many believe that some children are born to succeed in schools, others to fail, and the rest will lie somewhere along that continuum. For some parents and teachers the greatest fear is not that a student will fail but that he will fail and be judged a failure. When a student fails, we feel compelled to help him overlook his failure. Doing well in school seems less important than feeling good in school.

The opportunities to learn in American schools today, without any further reform at all, are tremendous. Immigrant students from certain parts of Asia are performing far above the norm in American schools. Why? Are they born smarter? There is no evidence that Asian students as a group are more gifted at birth. Nor are they usually favored economically or socially. They simply work harder than most native-born American kids. Most Americans apparently believe that success in school is mainly a result of genetics; Asian parents and their children believe it is primarily a result of hard work. Asian students lose self-esteem when they fail, because it means they did not work as hard as necessary.

Fortunately, most young people do eventually wake up and stop drifting. When they land a challenging job, most work as hard and perform as well as others. And the majority who find their way into college will be challenged by academic work and, by the time they graduate, perform at levels equivalent to students from other countries.

One American problem is that we condone and encourage a belief that adolescence is a period in one's life when it is natural and acceptable that a person should lack purpose, be irresponsible, lazy, and narcissistic. No other country has the same attitude toward its youth, at least to the same degree.

All of the above statements provide good reasons why it is harder to teach today than ever before. But these reasons cannot become excuses. The job of the teacher is to inspire and help learners to learn, whatever factors may be inhibiting learning. We live in a time when in addition to greater challenges to schools, there are also more opportunities. Teaching in the Information Age need not be as it was in the past; it can be more interesting and much more productive.

Learning in the Information Age

What do we know about learning? Quite frankly, we don't know enough, but we know much more than we knew even a decade ago.

It is difficult to study the mind and how it works. We can draw conclusions from experiments on animals; we can also make inferences from dissections of the human brain and from observing people and asking why they did what they do. But the brain—a marvelous organ possessed by every human being—continues to defy our ability to understand exactly how it works. For example, we don't know what happens in our brain when we have an inspiration or finally understand a complex equation. Neuroscientists are rather certain that inside each of our heads are 100 billion to a trillion neurons, constantly forging new connections and unraveling old ones in responses to messages from our senses. Somehow the brain connects one neuron to another creating circuitry that corresponds to patterns in the outside world. It seeks patterns among patterns, calls up stored information, and somehow we *understand*. We know it happens but we know very little about how it happens.

However, what we think about the mind may make a difference for instructional purposes. If we think of the mind as a kind of muscle, as many did at the turn of the century, then it doesn't matter much what we teach; we simply want to *stretch it* and give it exercise. At one time we taught

Latin in school, not because it was going to be very useful to most students, but because Latin was a difficult subject and required memorization of rules. We thought it would "toughen" the mind.

People have often thought of the student's mind as a kind of chest with many drawers. The task of teachers was to fill each of the drawers with appropriate content. Therefore, there was the English drawer, the history drawer, the math drawer, and so on. Perhaps a student would not need to open a drawer for decades, but someday he would need to know some obscure piece of information about ancient Egypt for example, and he would be able to open the mind's history drawer and find it.

For the past two decades the most common metaphor for the mind has been the computer, able to record and store information, and programmed to retrieve data when the proper commands are used. Computers can do routine things rapidly and consistently, not unlike the tasks people perform as matters of habit. And computers are able to *learn* in the sense that they can acquire new information and make connections to already stored information, as humans do.

But it is not useful to carry the analogy too far. The human mind is capable of feats well beyond any existing computer. Nevertheless, it is important to know that while our understanding and appreciation of the character and capacity of the human mind continues to grow, we are only beginning to learn how it actually operates.

Learning, like breathing, is a natural act. Most children and adults do not have to be coerced to learn. They enjoy learning. People will work very hard and even put themselves at risk to learn something they want to do. I remember vividly how I first learned to ride a bicycle. I was probably six or seven years old, and although I had no bicycle of my own, I was desperate to learn to ride. One day, some older boys placed me on one of their bikes and pushed me down a hill. I had watched them ride and knew I had to pedal. I was both excited and frightened because I had no idea what I should do to stop myself and dismount from the bike. As the bike slowed down, there was nothing to do but crash. Later, I learned other skills associated with bicycling, but I shall never forget the first time I rode a bike. Nearly everyone can relate similar stories of powerful learning moments.

Learning can seem nearly effortless. Children learn to walk and to talk with no formal instruction at all. They simply learn by observing and listening to others. Learning can also be very hard as when an adult tries to learn a foreign language or a new dance step. In these cases, learning which in other situations seems easy and normal may require special tutoring.

To say someone has learned something is to state that the individual can do something that they were not able to do before learning it. The learner can conjugate verbs, add fractions, explain the causes of the American Civil

"Mr. Stein makes us memorize stuff. We call him 'King of the Rote.'"

War, distinguish one impressionist painter from another, and so on. To have been merely in the presence of a teacher who had that information or knowledge doesn't count. A student who says, "I have learned French," means something different from the student who says, "I *took* French I and II in high school." Unfortunately too much of schooling is about taking courses rather than about learning.

When does it count that I have learned something? If I learned it for the test but can no longer remember it, did I learn it and then forgot it; or, if it is forgotten, did I ever truly learn it at all? Experts may disagree, but surely what schools should be interested in is long-term use of knowledge, rather than the kind of learning rewarded by examinations that favor short-term memory and low retention.

There is much we do not understand about learning. To what degree are some people born with greater capacity to learn than others? How important is experience in cultivating the intellect? How crucial are the early years of a child's development? Do boys learn differently from girls? Do some of us naturally learn in ways different from others or are these cultivated skills?

These and other questions have not been adequately resolved. All bear on the ways in which we organize and operate our schools. But we already know more about how youngsters learn than we are using. For our schools to improve, we must begin to draw upon the results of studies by cognitive scientists and learning psychologists.

Three Learning Theories from the Recent Past

Although the "chest of drawers" metaphor seems to be the operating model for many teachers, many theories of learning have been tested in schools since World War II. Three of the most important are behaviorism, mastery learning, and inquiry learning.

Behaviorism. Behaviorism is frequently associated with the Russian I. P. Pavlov and the American psychologist B. F. Skinner.[1] The principles of behaviorism grew out of experiments with animals. Animals were trained by a stimulus-response methodology, rewarded for correct behavior and punished for bad behavior. Reward came often in the form of food; punishment in the form of an electric shock. Because human beings are also pleasure-seeking, pain-avoidance animals, it seemed reasonable that the same techniques could be applied to them. Parents use behaviorism to arouse fear in young children of objects that could hurt them—touching a stove or wandering into a busy street. Teachers often apply behavioral techniques for classroom control.

Behaviorism influenced the development of programmed learning. If one can train an animal by breaking down complex tasks into simple ones and reinforce success as the animal progresses, behaviorists believe that human beings can also learn better if tasks leading to new knowledge are analyzed and appropriately sequenced.

Behavioral objectives were popular in schools three decades ago. Teachers and course designers would carefully specify the objectives to be accomplished by instruction, develop tests that were fair measures of the objectives, and then design instruction that would lead to successful performance on the tests. Even today remedial instruction in school draws largely upon behaviorist principles.

Behaviorism assumes that the teacher or the instructional designer knows exactly what is to be learned and can lead the student to gain control of the requisite knowledge. Behavioral approaches to instruction have been widely employed in the military and in corporate education. While behavioral approaches enjoyed brief popularity in schools, they have less impact on schooling today except for the teaching of handicapped and at-risk children.

Mastery Learning. The person most identified with mastery learning is Benjamin Bloom, a psychologist at the University of Chicago.[2] Bloom argued that within any particular population of learners, nearly anyone can learn what is required if given enough time and instruction. What happens in school is that only a specified amount of time is set aside to teach a topic: Some students learn what is required within the specified time; others don't. In most classrooms the consequences are that everyone must advance to the next topic, even though success in learning the next topic is dependent upon competence in the preceding one. Thus students who have failed to understand fully the first topic are certain to fail the second as well. According to Bloom, it is not that such students are unable to learn; they merely need more time, more tutoring, and/or more practice to reach the same level as their classmates. When we do not allow time for further work but move students along at the same assembly-line speed, the grading system we employ mainly reflects speed of learning rather than learning capability. The school has failed to perform its role, and the student who could have learned if given enough time and attention was cheated.

Mastery learning has been tested in a variety of settings and has proved remarkably successful. Nevertheless, it is used only rarely in American schools for two main reasons: flexibility of time and problems of grading.

For the typical teacher, the principles of mastery learning present an enormous challenge. Imagine a classroom of 24 students who are enrolled in a freshman algebra course. Following the first exam, it is apparent that half of the class seems to have understood the material; the remaining 12 students have varying levels of difficulty. The instructor has a problem. She needs to go on to the next task with the 12 successful students, but she should re-teach the earlier material to the 12 who failed to perform adequately. If this were not complicated enough, the 12 failing students require different amounts of assistance. Some can be brought up to the expected level within a day; others may require two or more days of further instruction before they have *mastered* the material. How does one teacher with 24 students who are operating at many levels of understanding handle the logistics of instruction? Time is a factor over which teachers have little control.

The second problem concerns grading. According to Bloom, schools tend to grade students on how quickly they learn something rather than if they learn it. If it takes one person two weeks to master something that only requires another individual one week, the students differ on their speed of learning but both have *mastered* the content. Therefore, there should be no distinction in how they are recognized by the school. But schools have trouble with this idea.

In the 1960s, John Patrick and I applied some of the ideas associated with behaviorism and mastery learning to a new high school civics course, *American Political Behavior (APB)*. While we were unable to implement the ideas fully, we were clear about the objectives, and the tests were designed to measure lesson objectives. We also encouraged teachers to believe that all students could *master* the course content. In keeping with Bloom's advice, we provided backup examinations that measured the same learning objectives as did the first test. We told the teachers that when students failed to reach mastery on the first examination (usually defined as 90 percent of answers correct), they should analyze the students' weaknesses, give them a chance to restudy the material they failed to understand, and take a backup exam. While this was less than a faithful representation of mastery learning, it approximated the spirit of the Bloom model.

At one level the idea was successful beyond our expectations. Students who failed the first exam did very well on the second exam. The problem was grading. The teachers said, "If we do as you suggest, we shall have to give nearly all of our students A's or B's, because all or nearly all are mastering the material on the second exam. However, our department chair (or principal) will not permit us to give such a high proportion of A's or B's. We can't count success on the second exam as equivalent to success on the first exam." Thus, the idea essentially failed in school because it ran counter to a school culture that assumes a normal distribution of success from instruction. Some students are expected to do poorly; the grading system proves our expectations to be correct. The APB teachers continued to use the backup tests, but not as we had hoped; they were used as makeup tests for students who were absent at the time the first test administration occurred.

Ideas promoted by behaviorism and mastery learning have had unanticipated effects on school practice. Behaviorism urged teachers to specify the outcomes of instruction and to teach for the test; mastery learning suggested that nearly all students could learn if given sufficient time and opportunity. In the 1970s these ideas contributed to the "minimal competency" movement, an effort to specify the most basic knowledge and skills one needed to survive in American society. Such competencies included the ability to read a bus schedule and to complete an IRS 1066 tax form. The assumption was that all high school graduates must be able to accomplish at least these minimal competencies; some students might go much beyond them. Because these competencies could not be achieved without instruction, the net effect was to "dumb down" the curriculum, leaving nearly everyone dissatisfied with the results.

However, the notion of focusing on results did not go away. Throughout the 1980s and early 1990s, various business and government leaders urged that the focus of school reform should be on the outcomes of instruction and the standards should become world class academic standards rather than minimal competence.

Outcomes-based education (OBE) has been growing rapidly. The Education Commission of the States reported in 1993 that 25 states had developed or implemented an outcome-based approach to education, and that 11 other states had made outcomes part of the state accreditation or assessment process.[3] Outcomes-based education has also become very controversial, in part because it is difficult to specify outcomes in a concrete matter without offering huge lists of items to be learned. The effect is to trivialize instruction. On the other hand, specifying outcomes in a more general way—e.g., students will act as responsible citizens—results in statements that are subject to wide interpretation that cannot be measured easily. But triviality and vagueness are not the only problems OBE faces. Some advocates of outcomes-based education have been attacked by both liberal and conservative critics. Some liberal educators oppose the specification of objectives because they believe they restrict learning; conservatives object because some of the outcomes are aimed at influencing attitudes and behavior as well as knowledge based upon academic disciplines. The conservatives believe that affective domains should be left to homes and religious institutions.

Inquiry Learning. Inquiry learning was popular in the late 1950s and throughout the 1960s. It took many forms according to various school subjects, but certain core ideas appeared in nearly all of the new curricula. One was an idea expressed by the Harvard University psychologist Jerome Bruner, the leader of the inquiry learning movement: "Any idea or problem or body of knowledge can be presented in a form simple enough so that any particular learner can understand it in a recognizable form."[4] This notion led to the restructuring of school curricula so that complex concepts and generalizations were introduced into the early grades with examples young students could understand. The second idea was that school courses should be organized according to the structure of the academic disciplines. Structure was also defined variously, but the most popular application was to organize the material around key concepts and generalizations used by experts in the discipline. The third idea was that students learn best if they employ the methods of inquiry used by research scholars in each discipline. A student would not merely learn what scholars had learned; he would *discover* the information himself, using methods analogous to those of the scholar.

American Political Behavior, mentioned earlier, was designed according to these theories. The political behavior approach to the study of politics was then the dominant one in the political science discipline; it presented a sharp contrast to the traditional approach to civics and government instruction in schools. The course focused on key concepts used by scholars, and students were frequently led to discover their own information using approaches similar or identical to those used by political behavioralists.

For example, one lesson used 12 political symbols to introduce the concepts of political culture and political socialization. Students were shown twelve, 35-mm slides. Each slide symbolized a political idea, a nation, or a political party. Some examples were a picture of the Statue of Liberty, a Nazi flag, the flag of the USSR, and a donkey as the symbol of the Democratic Party. Students were given a Likert scale and asked to record how they *felt* as they saw each symbol appear on the screen. Did they have a very bad feeling, a bad feeling, little or no feeling, a good feeling, or a very good feeling? The lesson was highly predictable, yielding similar outcomes whenever it was employed with students or adults. American symbols such as the Statue of Liberty produced uniformly "very good feeling" responses. Symbols clearly recognized as *the enemy*—e.g., USSR flag—produced "very bad feelings." Those that were recognizable but more complex—e.g., the symbol of the Democratic Party—produced mixed responses given the direction and level of partisanship of the students; and those they did not recognize at all—e.g., the Egyptian flag—produced "little or no feeling."

Once the students had completed their individual responses, their opinions were gathered, quickly tabulated by the teacher, and the classroom results formed the topic of student discussion. The questions from the teacher and answers from the students might proceed as follows (although greatly abbreviated here):

Teacher: Why did you indicate that the USSR flag gave you a "very bad feeling"?

Students: Because the USSR is our enemy, and they are trying to destroy our way of life.

Teacher: Why did you mark the Egyptian flag "little or no feeling"?

Students: Because we didn't recognize it and didn't know how to respond except for its color.

Teacher: If I showed the same slides to other American students do you think they would react as you did?

Students: Sure. There may be some differences, but Americans are likely to react to these symbols in the same way.

Teacher: Suppose I showed these same symbols to Russian students who are the same age as you. Would they react in the same way?

Students: No, of course not. They would love the Russian flag and have "very good feelings" for it; they would likely hate the picture of the Statue of Liberty and have "very bad feelings" toward that symbol.

Teacher: Why do you think all American students would think alike, but you and the Russians would be totally different?

Students: That's easy. They have been taught to hate the United States. That is what they learn from their government, from their parents, from their teachers, and from the mass media.

Teacher:	How did you learn your attitudes?
Students:	[Usually a long pause, then ...] From our parents? from mass media? from our teachers? from our government?
Teacher:	These are interesting hypotheses. During the next week you will have an opportunity to investigate to what degree these and other sources of information influence your political beliefs.

The purpose of the lesson was to make students sensitive to their own political attitudes and how they might be formed. In the weeks ahead they would review studies on the impact of various information sources, and they would begin to acquire new terms such as political culture and political socialization.

"New math," "new science," "new social studies," etc., which is what these new inquiry-oriented courses were called, made a big impact on schools in the 1960s but by the mid-1970s little trace could be found of them. They did not permanently replace the standard curricula, although some of the instructional ideas were picked up by publishers of traditional textbooks. Despite enormous sums of money spent on the development and distribution of the materials, the many hours devoted to retraining teachers to use the materials, and all of the public relations funds used to promote the products, the inquiry approach failed. Why? There are many explanations but some of the most widely accepted are: The new materials were too different from what the schools were accustomed to using; they placed too great a demand on teachers who lacked the time and training to fully understand them; they lacked support of parents who did not understand the content of courses and were threatened by them; they cost too much; the content did not align well with tests teachers were used to giving.

One criticism that was difficult to overcome was that true discovery was rarely possible. Students and teachers were limited to the materials that accompanied the project materials. The investigation was always circum- scribed by the materials available; "guided discovery" was provided instead of open-ended discovery. The teacher became bored with instruction after a time because the results of the inquiry were predictable. Inquiry exercises also began to bore students. Finally, the argument that underlay the entire approach—students should employ the methods of the scientist in order to understand the discipline—was ultimately rejected. Teachers were not con- vinced that the best way for students to learn was to have them act as scholars, especially if they had no intention of becoming academic scholars.

Some Recent Theories of Learning

New theories concerning learning are finding their way into schools. To a degree they are based upon earlier learning theories; they also share key assumptions with each other. The three theories described below support the view that schools should primarily promote reflection and higher-order thinking skills. While the proponents of these theories would likely acknowledge that other forms of learning are important, they favor those that promote learning in depth over approaches that support short-term memory. They are the theories of multiple intelligence, anchored instruction and situated cognition, and constructivism.

Theory of Multiple Intelligences. Strictly speaking, the theory of multiple intelligences (MI) is more a theory about intelligence than a theory of learning, but the theory has powerful implications for learning theory and for instruction and is therefore included in this group. MI is most closely associated with Howard Gardner, whose book, *Frame's of Mind: The Theory of Multiple Intelligences,* sets forth the main ideas relating to this theory.[5]

Gardner's research led him to the conclusion that human beings do not have a single, general intelligence but at least seven distinct and separate forms of intelligence. They are linguistic intelligence, logical-mathematical intelligence, spatial intelligence, musical intelligence, bodily-kinesthetic intelligence, and two forms of personal intelligence: interpersonal intelligence and intrapersonal intelligence. The first, linguistic intelligence, may be the one we know best; it involves ability to read and understand language and to use language eloquently. The second, logical-mathematical intelligence, is the intelligence used by people when they employ mathematics and science. Gardner notes that these two forms of intelligence are the ones that gain most of the attention; they are the substance of I.Q. and SAT tests. In general, academic courses stress linguistic intelligence and logical-mathematical intelligence.

Spatial intelligence provides a person with the capacity to form mental models of the relationship of objects in space and the ability to manipulate objects in space. Architects, for example, exhibit this intelligence. Musical intelligence speaks for itself; composers and performers have it in an abundance. Bodily-kinesthetic intelligence is the ability to perform tasks that require coordination of all parts of the body; athletes clearly exploit such intelligence, but dancers and dentists depend upon keen body coordination also. Interpersonal intelligence is the ability to understand other people, an ability required of ministers, counselors, and politicians. Intrapersonal intelligence is the capability to think clearly about oneself, to reflect objectively and be guided by one's observations. Although all of us possess capabilities in all seven areas, we are likely to differ greatly in which intelligences are most developed. It is not enough to say someone is very intelligent. We should ask, "Intelligent in what way?" Musical intelligence, spatial intelligence, and intrapersonal intelligence, to mention only three, are also forms of intelligence and deserve our attention and respect.

Gardner believes that everyone has the capacity to develop all seven intelligences, although it is likely true that we are genetically inclined to favor one or two over others. Surely our environment influences the development of each intelligence. A child born to musicians is more likely to exhibit musical intelligence than is a child who rarely if ever hears music performed live, at home or elsewhere. It is also likely that once a child experiences success in one domain, for example athletics, and earns recognition for his achievements, he is inclined to work further in that sphere. It is also likely that some intelligences reinforce one another; for example interpersonal and intrapersonal intelligence may promote each other's development.

Gardner argues that one purpose of school is to help young people grow in all seven intelligences; another purpose is to help students develop those intelligences that provide them with the greatest pleasure and satisfaction and will lead to career goals affording them the best opportunity to contribute productively to society. Such a school would have to give much greater attention to the individual and differential development of its students than is true of nearly all public schools today; a school would also need to accept that people do not learn in the same way, and that no one can learn everything. If Gardner's views were fully employed, not only would students differ greatly in what they got from school, but schools would also vary among themselves. This approach would also greatly complicate national examinations.

Anchored Instruction and Situation Cognition. These two ideas have been joined for this discussion because they share common assumptions and beliefs. However, they also are being developed by different groups of researchers. Situated cognition is perhaps most closely associated with John Seely Brown and Paul Duguid of the Institute on Learning in Palo Alto, and with Allan Collins a research scientist at Bolt, Beranek, and Newman.[6] Anchored instruction is most closely identified with the Cognition and Technology Group at Vanderbilt University headed by John Bransford.[7]

Both groups are concerned with the problem of inert knowledge. Inert knowledge is knowledge one possesses, has stored in the mind, and might recall when asked to do so; however, inert knowledge is often not used spontaneously to solve problems even when it would be relevant to do so. For example, algebra and geometry might prove useful when calculating how many rolls of wallpaper will be required to cover the walls of a room. But it is also likely that most people will no longer remember the formulas they once knew that would help them, and they will make do with simple arithmetic.

In contrast to inert knowledge is the notion of knowledge as a tool. Just as we select a tool—a screwdriver, hammer, pliers—to assist us in performing a particular task, knowledge should be called upon to help us solve particular problems. Learning should be organized so that students acquire tool knowledge.

The problem of school, in the minds of Brown, Bransford, and others who work with them, is that school imposes its own culture on learning. The results are two domains of learning: One consists of school-based activities; the second is authentic activities, or learning in a real-life situation where one needs and uses knowledge. For example, children acquire their own language quite easily from living at home and playing with their peers. Vocabulary and grammar structure are reproduced as they hear it. The activities are authentic. As children grow older, the school tries to teach them a foreign language or attempts to expand their English vocabulary by adding words they rarely, if ever, use. The result is hours of agony and frustration for both the teacher and the learners.

While all good teachers try to relate their instruction to real world experience in order to make the lesson relevant, the two research groups want to go beyond these traditional classroom applications. Vanderbilt researchers have created instructional episodes that pose problems to fictitious characters portrayed in each episode. One set of exercises is built around the exploits of Sherlock Holmes, a second around a fictitious character named Jasper Woodbury. The Jasper Woodbury series uses problems faced by the hero that must be solved by applying a mathematical formula. Problems are presented in a videodisc format, so that the student can return to the problem again and again, or simply study some features in depth. The researchers also use videodiscs because they approximate the media format preferred by young people today. By presenting real problems, although fictionalized, that are like the problems the students might face if they were in Jasper Woodbury's situation, the researchers hope to make the activity authentic and the resultant learning a more powerful tool for the students.

Those working in situated cognition are puzzling over the same issues of how to overcome inert knowledge. They have drawn attention to the differences that exist between school-based learning and learning one gains as an apprentice. An apprentice, while a novice, is constantly attempting to develop his knowledge and skill to resemble that of the expert under whose supervision he is working. To Brown and others, school should try to make novices more like experts in each academic domain.

A part of their solution resembles closely the line of argument presented by advocates of inquiry learning in the 1960s. They believe that students should be exposed to the conceptual tools of the various academic disciplines and solve real-world problems as would mathematicians, scientists, or historians. This is similar to the "structure of the discipline" approach described earlier.

They have coined the term "cognitive apprentice." A cognitive apprentice places himself in a novice-to-master relationship to an expert in an academic discipline, just as novice carpenters have been apprenticed to master carpenters. One way of implementing this relationship is for students to generate real world problems in mathematics, for example, and observe how their mathematics teacher solves them. Students might identify social problems for study in social studies classes and participate as their teacher tries to solve the problem with them.

Anchored instruction and situated cognition have important implications for curricula and how we organize schools.

Constructivism. Constructivism poses the largest challenge to schools and to the current reform movement because it questions ordinary conceptions of knowledge, familiar instructional approaches, and the most widely used forms of student testing.[8]

Constructivists begin with nontraditional ideas about the nature of knowledge and the learning process. For them, knowledge is not something that exists independently of human beings, nor is the process of learning one of implanting information into students' minds—putting it in their mental "dresser drawers." They argue that learning is a constructive process in which the learner constructs his own understanding of the object. There can be no learning unless the learner is actively engaged in creating his own representation of knowledge.

For example, assume a world history classroom in which a teacher asks students to learn that "Rome fell in 476 A.D." In some classes, merely remembering the date will be sufficient for the examination; in others students will be expected to associate the *fall of Rome* with the ascension to power of Romulus Augustulus. But what does the phrase, "Rome fell in 476 A.D." mean to a 15-year-old, tenth-grade world history student? Probably not what the textbook author or his history teacher thinks it means. First, the student came to the class with a concept of falling; so when he adds the new information he has recently acquired about Rome, he may visualize a city collapsing into a heap of rubble throughout that year. What can he possibly know of the year 476 A.D.? He knows it was a long time ago, but beyond that, what does he know? Because his experience is different from others, his interpretation is likely to be different from others in his class, from his teacher, and certainly from historians of the Roman Empire. A test question that asks, "When did Rome fall?," may well obtain the right answer. But if the teacher begins to probe what the answer means to him, she would likely be surprised and greatly disappointed.

According to constructivists, it is not only the naive student who has a distorted impression of the factual statement. So do his teachers, and the scholar who wrote the textbook. Even if one had lived during the period itself, it would have been impossible to know the meaning of the phrase in the same way as others living at the same time. What we know of the world consists of human interpretations of reality. Therefore all knowledge statements are at best approximations of objective knowledge.

The teacher's task, from a constructivist point of view, is to resist the tendency to draw ideas based upon her knowledge and experience, the curriculum guide, or textbook and attempt to implant them into the minds of her students. She must begin with the students' minds and the knowledge they bring to her class, helping them construct a meaningful interpretation of the new information.

For example, here are some statements from fifth and sixth graders showing their understanding of science. Presumably, they had acquired information from the teacher or textbook and tried to make sense of it.[9]

"Most books now say our sun is a star. But it still knows how to change back into a sun in the daytime."

"Many dead animals in the past changed to fossils while others preferred to be oil."

"Some oxygen molecules help fires burn while others help make water, so sometimes it's brother against brother."

"When they broke open molecules, they found they were only stuffed with atoms. But when they broke open the atoms, they found them stuffed with explosions."

These statements made sense to the students as they fit their frame of reference. It should be obvious that teaching students science by simply insisting that they be able to recall certain words and phrases will produce results like these. In order to make sense of the new information, the student must make the new information fit logically into his perspective.

Adopting a constructivist view requires a fundamental change in the way teachers approach instruction. First, it is as important to know one's students as individuals as it is to know one's subject; second, the teacher must allow time to study selected topics in depth; third, learners must be encouraged to explore widely as they try to build their own interpretation of the topics; and fourth, teachers must become learners themselves, in part to model the process but also to understand more fully the student experience.

It should be obvious that traditional views of testing seem silly, unfair, and pointless from the constructivist point of view. Equally suspect is the notion of *core knowledge*, if by that phrase one means the ability of each student to represent faithfully what is *known* about events, people, and times.

What Do We Know about Learning?

As noted earlier, we know a great deal about how people learn, more than we used to, but not enough to provide prescriptions for teachers. One complication is that the learning tasks confronting students are not all of a kind. For some purposes, behavioral principles are appropriate—e.g., learning how to assemble a complex piece of machinery. It is not necessary to have multiple perspectives on the machine or to discover how to assemble it through a discovery process. Following clear directions and assembling the parts in a sequenced, programmed order provides the most efficient and satisfying method to the learner.

Mastery learning also is important to classroom instruction. Learning rules of grammar, for example, is a task that can take many forms, but there are correct and incorrect ways to use any language. Students must learn the rules and apply them in many new situations. Effective instruction often involves drill and practice: Students do not acquire language competence at the same speed, and time must be provided for the slow students to have additional opportunities for tutoring and practice while the swift go forward.

Inquiry-based learning and constructivist approaches are best employed in promoting higher-order thinking. Such thinking skills as analysis, synthesis, and evaluation require that students have the opportunity to form their own views and share their opinions with others. Drill and practice have been misapplied frequently in science and the humanities where more reflective approaches would be better.

The current emphasis among school reformers upon inquiry and problem solving skills, coupled with a constructivist point of view, stems from a reaction to recent school practices that have pushed students to perform well on examinations that reward short-term memory, and low-level thinking skills. Reform advocates believe that the higher-order skills have been neglected, making schools less interesting and challenging for students and depriving our society of adults who have been taught how to use their mental capacity to full advantage.

One point to remember is that there is no single theory of learning that fits all situations. Good teachers are guided by theories that fit the learning task and choose their pedagogical approach accordingly.

Theories of Teaching

Teaching and learning are the yin and yang of education. In the best of circumstances the two fit tightly together, so closely that the boundaries between them are barely discernible. The highest compliment a teacher can receive from a learner is, "You made this so easy that I was able to learn it by myself."

There is little value in a theory of teaching that is unconnected to a theory of learning, for it is the teacher's job to adapt instruction to the learner rather than require the learner to adapt to the teacher. If, for example, we believed that shouting at students, scolding them when they offer unique solutions, and punishing them for failure were ways students learn best, then we would shout, scold, employ sarcasm, and punish them. Indeed, these techniques are employed from time to time, especially by athletic coaches, although they would appear to be counter productive.

Much is written about various teaching styles. Teachers vary in the teaching tasks they like most and do best: lecture, lead discussion, devise interesting activities, consult with students, etc. Teachers are also encouraged to lead from their strengths. Unfortunately, there is both value as well as the opportunity for error in the notion of teaching styles. A teacher may believe that she is a great lecturer, may enjoy preparing lectures, and may be praised by colleagues for the quality of her lectures; but if students fail to learn from the lectures, she is a bad teacher. The purpose of schooling is not to encourage and support brilliant teacher performances. It is to ensure extraordinary learning.

New teachers fear most of all their ability to control classroom behavior and to manage instruction so that students are constantly busy. Veteran teachers give new teachers tips for accomplishing these goals. "Don't smile until Christmas," "Start hard and ease up later," "Give them lots of worksheets to fill out in class and have students grade each other's work": These and other *tips* are some of the advice I received when I began to teach. These tips are a kind of folk culture that is passed from one generation of teachers to the next. Arguably such ideas may help maintain classroom control and keep students busy. Beyond creating the minimal conditions for learning, however, they have little to do with good instruction. Unfortunately, some teachers never go beyond these methods of classroom control and fail to become the teachers they might have been. Most teachers overcome their initial fears, create interesting conditions for learning, win the respect of their students, and thus *control* their classrooms by the challenging and interesting instruction they provide.

Principles of Teaching

Successful reform of American schools will require making the teaching/learning process more effective on the whole than it has been. We must begin to apply what we know about how students learn and tailor our instruction to fit the learning process.

In 1993 the Presidential Task Force on Psychology in Education of the American Psychological Association produced a document called *Learner-*

centered psychological principles: Guidelines for school redesign and reform.[10] These principles draw upon the most widely promoted theories of learning today and are intended to offer guidance for teachers. According to the task force, the principles are consistent with more than a century of research and with best practice in schools.

In the pages that follow I shall quote the principle contained in the task force report, then offer my own commentary regarding how these principles might affect instruction. There are twelve principles in all. The first ten principles are subdivided into four groups: metacognitive and cognitive factors, affective factors, development factors, and personal and social factors; the remaining two focus on individual differences and relate to all of the preceding ten.

Principle 1. The Nature of the Learning Process. *Learning is a natural process of pursuing meaningful goals, and it is active, volitional, and internally mediated; it is a process of discovery and constructing meaning from information and experience, filtered through the learner's unique perceptions, thoughts, and feelings.*

Students learn easily and naturally and will persist at difficult tasks that are interesting and relevant to them. They are also capable of assuming responsibility for their learning when the teacher designs instruction so as to encourage and facilitate self-directed learning.

Teachers can be deceived into thinking that because they are giving students much information, the students must be learning a great deal. Not true—or at least not necessarily true. The students may not even be listening to the teacher, let alone processing the new information. Teachers must find ways that engage students in tasks that challenge them intellectually and are intrinsically interesting. The teacher's role then becomes one of assisting, counseling, or coaching students when help is needed.

In general, the most important and demanding part of a teacher's role is planning and preparing for instruction—precisely the part that is least recognized and respected by the lay public. American teachers spend more hours with their students on any given school day than do teachers in any other industrialized nation; yet many school critics believe teachers have it easy because they only *teach* six hours per day, referring only to the hours they are with students. Instruction is not likely to improve until teachers are provided more time and better conditions in which to prepare for instruction. Learning is more likely to be fun, interesting, and challenging to students when teachers have had adequate time to make it so.

Principle 2. Goals of the Learning Process. The learner seeks to create meaningful, coherent representations of knowledge regardless of the quantity and quality of the data available.

Students are driven to make sense of new information, even if they don't fully understand it. They integrate the new information with their existing theories of knowledge so that it seems internally consistent. The result can be nonsense, but it makes sense to the learner. This means that a teacher must know her students well, not only as a group but as individuals; otherwise she can only guess at the conclusions they have reached from her instruction. As a result, teachers must provide students with opportunities for them to share their understanding orally, in writing, or through some other medium in order that she can recognize each student's perspective and help the student make modifications as needed. Unless the teacher creates opportunities for feedback, beyond the use of short-answer examinations, she has no idea what students have grasped.

Principle 3. The Construction of Knowledge. *The learner links new information with existing and future-oriented knowledge in uniquely meaningful ways.*

Each student brings a unique background and experience to the classroom that leads him to employ new information in ways that are special to him. Many teachers behave as if the information they are providing is being processed by students in the same way, leaving them with an understanding identical to that of each other and the teacher. But this is not how it works at all. The fact that differing responses occur should be seen as an asset for instruction rather than a liability to be overcome. Teachers should take advantage of the students' various interpretations by engaging them in discourse with one another. This not only provides the students with the opportunity to share their beliefs but also to shape further their own beliefs by hearing their colleagues' perspectives. The result is a deeper, more complex understanding by pupils than if they were denied the opinions of their peers.

Principle 4. Higher Order Thinking. *Higher order strategies for "thinking about thinking"—for overseeing and monitoring mental operations—facilitate creative and critical thinking and the development of expertise.*

If there is anything on which all of the reformers agree, it is that schools must cultivate higher-order thinking skills on the part of all of their students, not merely the academically talented. Higher-order thinking includes not only such skills as analysis, synthesis, and evaluation; it also includes the ability to think about thinking, what psychologists call metacognitive or executive level of thinking. By early to middle childhood, students can be made aware of their own process of thinking and how they can take charge of making themselves better thinkers. Currently, only the best students become reflective about their own learning, giving them even further advantages over their less capable peers. Teachers need to design instruction so that all students become more skilled at learning.

Often, schooling seems designed to make students dependent upon teachers; schools should be structured to help students become independent learners. In order to assist students in the process of self-learning, teachers must plan lessons that encourage problem solving, critical thinking, and individual investigations that provide students with practice in thinking for themselves.

Principle 5. Motivational Influences of Learning. *The depth and breadth of information processed, and what and how much is learned and remembered, are influenced by (a) self-awareness and beliefs about personal control, competence, and ability; (b) clarity and saliency of personal values, interests, and goals; (c) personal expectations for success and failure; (d) affect, emotion, and general states of mind; and (e) the resulting motivation to learn.*

It is the teacher's job to create a classroom environment where students want to learn. Students should look forward to class because the work is stimulating; because the teacher is interesting, has a good sense of humor, knows her subject, and likes students; because the atmosphere is both fun and businesslike; and because the instructional materials are adequate to support inquiry. Teachers can further enhance student motivation by allowing students some choices in the topics to be studied and in how the topics will be investigated and finally assessed.

Principle 6. Intrinsic Motivation to Learn. *Individuals are naturally curious and enjoy learning, but intense negative cognitions and emotions (e.g., feeling insecure, worrying about failure, being self conscious or shy, and fearing corporal punishment, ridicule, or stigmatizing labels) thwart this enthusiasm.*

A student's ability to learn is greatly affected by his feelings and attitudes. By the time most teachers encounter students, they have already had considerable experience in school—some good and some bad. Some adolescents, for example, are painfully self-conscious about themselves within their peer group; some students have been led to think they are dumb and cannot learn; others have experienced having their ideas ridiculed in class. It is part of the teacher's job to help students gain confidence in their ability to learn and become independent thinkers. This may mean finding tasks that attract positive attention to shy students; it may mean scaling responsibilities for students who lack confidence, so that they have some success while they are preparing for more demanding work. This is not to be equated with the direction followed by some well-meaning but misguided teachers who decide certain students cannot learn, assign them trivial work, and praise them regardless of quality. Students are to be encouraged and helped to do their best, but not praised when their work is less than acceptable for them or any other student.

Principle 7. Characteristics of Motivation-enhancing Learning Tasks. *Curiosity, creativity, and higher-order thinking are stimulated by relevant, authentic learning tasks of optimal difficulty and novelty for each student.*

Perhaps, the most difficult job for teachers is to match learning tasks to the ability and interest of individual students. In the best circumstance, a teacher should have a wide range of activities ready to be undertaken with regard to any topic of study. The activities should be those that are within the ability of each learner, while challenging them to new levels of accomplishment. For example, students can gather information in many ways: reading their textbooks, conducting library research, interviewing people they know, interviewing public officials, and so on. Each method of gathering information demands a different level of skill and experience. Reporting the results of the study can also be scaled to levels of difficulty: providing a written summary of the findings for the teacher; organizing a panel to share results orally with the class; preparing an opinion piece for the local newspaper; and preparing a multimedia presentation on the findings for a service club. Each type of report has merit, but each requires different skills and levels of confidence. The teacher's job is to move students up the ladder of difficulty without overwhelming them or undermining their success.

The way in which the course of study is organized can also make a difference. Students are more interested in learning if they believe that what they are studying is linked to issues that matter. Problem-centered instruction that calls for real solutions on the part of students has more appeal than mere coverage of academic content. For example, making students responsible for planning an election campaign for a real candidate makes it necessary for them to cope with problems relating to campaign finance, responding to conflicting pressure group demands, the demographics of voter participation and other issues likely to be raised in an American Government course but treated in a more didactic, abstract way. When I was an American Government teacher 30 years go, I concluded the course with an extensive, international simulation that required students to develop economic, political, and military strategies for their own nation while negotiating and bargaining with presumed friendly and unfriendly nations. Not only was it a good way to keep seniors on task during the last weeks of the semester, but it also engaged their interest far beyond ordinary instruction and helped them understand the pressures and constraints faced by policy makers.

Principle 8. Developmental Constraints and Opportunities. *Individuals progress through stages of physical, intellectual, emotional, and social development that are a function of unique genetic and environmental factors.*

Teachers are generally aware that instruction should be designed to fit the developmental stages of their students. This has never been a simple task, but it has become more complex as a result of federal legislation calling for placing children who were once assigned solely to special education classrooms in regular classes. It is important to respect and accept differences while discouraging stigmatizing practices such as labeling students, organizing students by ability level, or holding students back to repeat a grade level. Teachers should encourage peer group and cross-age tutoring; these permit more advanced students to help those who are still struggling with new information and skills. Teachers should avoid instructional materials, designed for a single grade level, that are too easy for the best students and too difficult for slow-learning students.

Schools have not found it easy to address the problem of responding successfully to developmental differences. "Pull out classes," in which low ability students are taken out of regular classes to work on deficiencies, leave them further behind in their regular classes. Imposing high academic standards without providing adequate tutoring ensures further failure. Ungraded primary schools show promise for very young children; more individual options for high school students, including work apprenticeships and the opportunity to begin college courses for the most academically able, are some of the ways schools can respond to differences.

Principle 9. Social and Cultural Diversity. *Learning is facilitated by social interactions and communications with others in flexible, diverse (in age, culture, family background, etc.) and adaptive instructional settings.*

Classrooms can provide opportunities for students to learn from each other as well as from the teacher. Students in a typical school reflect a variety of race, ethnic, cultural, and social class backgrounds. Part of the justification for the American public school is to provide settings where people with different interests and experiences can interact. Good teachers will seek problems or topics that facilitate such dialogues without appearing to be doing so. Teachers should organize task groups that reflect diversity. One of the benefits of collaborative learning is the experience students acquire from working on a project together.

Principle 10. Social Acceptance, Self-esteem, and Learning. *Learning and self-esteem are heightened when individuals are in respectful and caring relationships with others who see their potential, genuinely appreciate their unique talents, and accept them as individuals.*

A teacher must set the tone for the class by making clear her own interest and concern for each student. Some students are easier to like than others, but the teacher must respect and care for all of her students. She must also establish norms that require students' respect for who they are and what they are able to contribute. Students cannot learn easily in settings where they think they are not valued.

Teachers can also undertake projects that help students serve others. Programs that permit students to volunteer for community service activities not only permit students to make positive contributions to their community but also gain the satisfaction from knowing that their work was needed, welcomed, and appreciated.

Principle 11. Individual Differences in Learning. *Although basic principles of learning, motivation, and effective instruction apply to all learners (regardless of ethnicity, race, gender, physical ability, religion, or socioeconomic status), learners have different capabilities and preferences for learning mode and strategies. These differences are a function of environment (what is learned and communicated in different cultures or other social groups) and heredity (what occurs naturally as a function of genes).*

Even within the siblings of a given family we can easily detect differences in how children and youth learn. Some children are cautious and avoid new experiences unless they are certain they will succeed, while others seem extremely bold and appear to learn best by trial and error. Some children prefer to read quietly on their own; others crave activity and interaction with others. If such differences exist within families, they are greatly expanded within any given classroom. The teacher's job is to take advantage of these differences, to respect them, and to help individual students to understand their learning preferences.

Principle 12. Cognitive Filters. *Personal beliefs, thoughts, and understanding resulting from prior learning and interpretations become the individual's basis for constructing reality and interpreting life experience.*

Teachers must deal with children from different cultural backgrounds from her own. These students may interpret her instruction quite differently than she intends, because of cultural differences. Teachers must also be alert to how cultural differences among students in class create misunderstanding and conflict. Part of her job is to help students understand how the process of socialization has led them to interpret life experiences; such instruction can enable students to overcome their socialization to a certain degree. There are risks to both the teacher and the class. A common issue facing teachers is how to handle content that challenges students' religious beliefs. For many students, topics such as evolution and abortion are not theoretical issues subject to debate. They hold deep-seated beliefs on these topics that have been cultivated at home and at church. To attack such beliefs is to threaten the students' identity. The multicultural nature of American classrooms has increased the complexity of the problem because other religious groups—Moslems, Hindus, Buddhists, for example—are also likely to be members of the class, along with Protestants, Catholics, and Jews.

A review of these 12 principles should make clear that good teaching requires more than knowledge of one's subject and a bag of pedagogical techniques. Good teaching begins with understanding one's students well; it depends upon the teacher's ability "to get inside each student's head" in order to see the world as they do; and it requires the skill to inspire, coax, and encourage students to work to their capacity.

Technology and Learning

Can technology become the key to improved learning? This depends on what else we do.

In 1983 Richard Clark published a review of research on the use of media to enhance learning. Clark concluded ". . . there are no learning benefits to be gained from employing any specific medium to deliver instruction"; he further concluded that ". . .media do not influence learning under any conditions" and that ". . .media are mere vehicles that deliver instruction but do not influence student achievement any more than the truck that delivers our groceries causes changes in our nutrition."[11] Although Clark found research that attempted to document the effectiveness of one media over another, when Clark looked beyond the conclusions to the nature of the experiment itself, it seemed clear to him that the variation in effect could usually be accounted for by the difference in instructional strategy employed in the study. Thus, if medium A used strategy X and medium B used strategy Y, Clark wrote that it was inappropriate to judge medium A as superior to B regardless of gains by students in the A group. The difference lay in the instructional strategy X as opposed to Y. Clark's opinion was very controversial and has been debated vigorously for more than a decade.[12]

Without attempting to settle the debate, let us assume for the moment that Clark is correct. Thus, it is not the technology that determines instructional effectiveness but the instructional strategy underlying the use of the media. This finding is very important because technology, when used appropriately, can be employed to make instruction more powerful than it would otherwise be. Thus, the answer is, "It all depends."

There is another way to think about the role technology may play in instruction; perhaps it will encourage teachers to undertake sound instructional practices that have been difficult to implement in the past. Consider the example of pen pals. For decades, foreign language teachers have urged their students to establish pen pals in the country that is the source for the foreign language they study. What is the impact of electronic mail on pen-pal relationships? On the one hand, we should expect no greater value to the student if the letter is received by postal mail or by electronic mail. Yet we know that electronic mail is quicker, and it is easier to maintain contact between the writers. Therefore, electronic mail should offer advantages over postal mail. A second example is based upon the instructional advantages students gain from participation in field trips. But field trips that travel great distance from school are hard to manage and finance. What if the field trips could be conducted live electronically to anywhere in the world? If Clark is right, the impact of the field trip could be the same—whether it is experienced in person or mediated by television. Electronically, students are able to take field trips to many more locations at much greater distance than before, thus enhancing learning.

Technology may also be used by reformers and teachers as a catalyst for change. While it may be true that nearly every powerful instructional strategy can be employed without technology, the effort to infuse technology into schools may encourage teachers to use more powerful instructional strategies, strategies they might have valued in the past but felt incapable of employing.

Finally, those who study learning emphasize the importance of making instruction authentic, dealing with real problems and making learning in school resemble learning outside of school as much as possible. What is authentic experience to young people today is not the same as that enjoyed by previous generations. Marketing specialists have coined the term "screenagers" to refer to young Americans who are 18 to 24 years old. Seventy percent of this age group uses a computer every day. They are as comfortable surfing the Internet as their parents are talking on the telephone. Technology is used extensively outside of school; by using technology within schools, we can make the conditions of school more authentic.

Conclusion

If a topic is likely to be taught only in school, then it must be taught there if we want students to have that information. One example is the periodic table of elements that is ordinarily a part of instruction in chemistry. It is doubtful that students will encounter such information outside of school. Other topics are taught outside of school, but schools provide instruction on these for their own purposes. Sex education is one example. It is unlikely that people would stop having babies if sex education were dropped from the school curriculum. Schools include sex education because school officials believe issues of health and safety relating to sexual practices are not likely to be treated well or will be overlooked by the media and other sources of information about sex. Thus, schools often supplement or correct information available from other sources.

Second, merely because something is taught does not mean it will be learned. Actually, it is not accurate to say something was taught but not learned; it is more correct to say it was *presented* or *covered* but neither taught nor learned. When teachers hurry to complete a lesson or sweep through a century of world history in order to *cover it,* they may satisfy their consciences that they have covered the material, but they are not likely to have taught it.

Third, *how* something is taught determines what will be learned. If we want students to understand mathematics, they must learn and be able to apply the principles, theories, and rules of mathematics. Memorizing the multiplication tables is undoubtedly useful, but it does not lead to under-standing mathematics. At one time, we taught poetry for the beauty and elegance of its language; students were often expected to recite poems on demand. Today we are more likely to "deconstruct" poetry, looking for hid-den meanings while seeking out the poet's biases and prejudices. These two ways to study poetry lead to quite different ends.

Fourth, individuals vary. They do not have the same background experi-ence, genes, ability, and interests; their development occurs at different rates, and they prefer to learn in ways different from others. In the best of cir-cumstances, all instruction is individualized, carefully matched to the abilities, interests, and needs of the learner. Except in special situations, schools have not been able to afford individualized tutoring and have settled for group instruction, accommodating individual differences as best they can.

And, finally, theories of learning, useful as they may be, remain theories of learning. We know more about how people learn than we use; we know less than would be useful to know. Most theories are limited to one or more aspects of learning; no single theory accounts for all that we may wish to accomplish in school. As a result, total commitment to any single theory will nearly always lead to ruin.

Chapter 4

TECHNOLOGY: THE KEY TO SCHOOL REFORM

Give me a place to stand and I will move the earth.
Archimedes (287-212 B.C.)

The successful transformation of student learning and accomplishment in the next decade requires effectively bringing together three agendas—an emerging consensus about learning and teaching, well-integrated uses of technology, and restructuring. Each agenda alone presents possibilities for educational redesign of a very powerful sort. Yet none has realized or is likely to realize its potential in the absence of the other two. Karen Sheingold. [1]

Archimedes was a great fan of the lever, a piece of technology that was presumably *state-of-the-art* when he lived. While not every person exhibits Archimedes' enthusiasm toward technology, before and since Archimedes, and throughout all regions of the earth, people have used technology to make their lives richer and more comfortable. Indeed, the ability to make and use such tools as the fulcrum and the lever is one of the ways we distinguish human beings from other species of animals.

Technology is not only a product of a given culture; it also shapes the culture. The automobile is not merely an American artifact; it influences where we live, where we work, how we entertain ourselves, and provides a statement to others about who we are. The automobile has affected courtship patterns and relationships among races and social classes. Getting a driver's license and acquiring a car is a rite of passage in American society. To a remarkable degree, while we make our tools, our tools also make us.

At first we may be unaware of how a particular culture is being affected by new technology. We may stretch conventional terms to fit the new phenomena because that is one way to be comfortable with it. For example, an early name for the car was horseless carriage, and we ask about the horsepower of gasoline-powered vehicles, as if we could imagine hitching 200 horses to the front of a car. Meanwhile, changes are occurring all around us that we barely notice. At first, the car is an object of humor; it frequently breaks down and when it does, people shout, "Get a horse." Then autos slowly become more dependable, and are purchased by wealthy people as a status symbol. Henry Ford decides cars can be made cheaply enough for nearly everyone to become an owner and proceeds to build them. Others follow his lead, and the car becomes something everyone requires. Horses become food for dogs.

Consider another example of how technology affects our lives. A part of the history of the Industrial Revolution was changes that occurred in England relating to the manufacture of cloth. At one time, wool spinning and looming were cottage industries. A middle man bought wool, took it to cottages where the raw wool was spun into thread and woven into cloth, and then transported the cloth to tailors and seamstresses who manufactured the finished product.

With the advent of water power and, later, steam power, it was possible to erect large factories near sources of power and labor and install huge spinning wheels and looms capable of producing cloth much quicker, less expensively, and of a higher dependable quality than could the hundreds of cottage workers.

Today, we are witnessing the return of another kind of cottage industry. It's called "telecommuting." In ever greater numbers, white collar workers are working out of their homes and cars, with the encouragement of their employers. In 1993, one survey found that of 100 companies contacted, 30 percent had some type of telecommuting in place. Large firms find it advantageous to reduce the number of offices they must maintain in expensive downtown locations; with the use of modern electronic tools that permit the office worker to communicate by voice and fax and with a modem to send and receive data by telephone, a worker can carry his office with him and be closer to his customer. Today, it can truly be said, by some, that if there is something really important to get done at the office, it's best to stay at home.

Technological changes do not benefit everyone. Blacksmiths and horses, for example, didn't fare so well earlier in the century. Sometimes people literally fight back. In the mid-nineteenth century, Ned Lud became so angry he smashed two textile frames belonging to his Leicestershire employer. Following his lead and taking his name, Luddites attacked the labor-saving machinery they saw threatening their pay and jobs. French workers followed suit; they resisted the Industrial Revolution by jamming sabots, their wooden shoes, into the spinning equipment that was stealing their jobs, thus giving rise to the term saboteurs. Nevertheless, the Luddites and the saboteurs lost, as resisters nearly always do when confronted with technology.

Today it seems rather simple to mark the changes that led to the Agriculture Revolution and the Industrial Revolution. But when one is in the midst of rapid change, it is more difficult to know when things started, when they peaked, and when they ended. The Industrial Revolution was named and described by twentieth century historians, not the ones who lived through it.

The pace of change is even faster today. For example, from the invention of the wheel up through the seventeenth and eighteenth centuries, people had no other means of land transportation other than walking, riding an animal, or being carried in a wagon pulled by an animal. In the nineteenth century, steam engines provided wagons with power, followed by gasoline-powered, internal combustion engines, followed by all the forms of powered vehicles we have today. In one generation, those Americans who once depended upon horses and walking for transportation learned to drive cars, flew on airplanes, and watched as rocket propulsion took men to the moon.

Consider human communication. The first was human speech that required human memory to maintain folk traditions. Then came writing in various forms: hieroglyphics, cuneiform, and alphabetic signs composed on many kinds of materials. Writing created a need for scribes, who maintained records for the rest of us. Then Johann Gutenberg began to print books, which in time made literacy a value within reach of many rather than the few, and we stored our memories in libraries. Today our culture is saved in electronic data bases.

Transportation and communication are the driving forces of the new age. They make it possible for us to maintain as close contact with friends abroad as the ones within our own communities. We can also know what is happening nearly anywhere in the world while it is occurring and sometimes to greater advantage than those who are present on the scene. A Russian friend told me that he followed the autumn 1993 assault on the Russian parliament building by watching it on CNN. Although he was in Moscow, he learned more from CNN than from being present where the event was occurring. Because CNN offices are less than a mile away from the Russian parliament, CNN cameramen were able to send vivid pictures of the assault not only around the world but back to Moscow for the best description of events while they were underway. Marshall McCluhan once described the earth as a global village; here was a splendid example of global village communication.

Modern transportation and communication helped break the back of the USSR and its hold on Eastern Europe. They have also forced changes in the way American firms do business. For many firms, it is no longer sensible to speak of domestic and nondomestic markets; buyers, sellers, manufacturers, laborers, and capital are global phenomena. America was the major force in creating the global economy; it must now live with the results.

Technology and Schooling

Technology has always been an important part of schooling in America; it is only that until now the technology employed was rather simple and changed slowly. No one reading this text can remember when there were no textbooks, but the kind of textbooks we have today are largely twentieth century products. Nor did teachers always have their primary tools—the blackboard and chalk. Slate blackboards did not appear in urban schools until the 1830s.

When I was a young boy, one of the rituals for starting school was a trip to the local department store to purchase school supplies: a "Big Chief" tablet, pencils, rubber erasers, pens with removable points (they became dull quickly), and a bottle of ink. Sometimes a pencil box would be added in order that I could keep track of my personal supplies. Parents and students today go through similar shopping rituals with the onset of school. The technology has changed somewhat (ball point pens have replaced ink and straight pens, pencil boxes have given way to backpacks), but the technology, although improved, is essentially the same.

There have been many attempts to change the technology of schooling. They have each appeared with great fanfare and expressions of optimism by their advocates. In the 1920s, radio was expected to have a major impact on schools; it was film in the 1930s, television in the 1950s, and teaching machines in the 1960s. The one piece of new technology from that era that truly found a place was the overhead projector. Introduced in the 1940s by the military, it gradually found its way into schools. It is easy to use and relatively inexpensive; it permits the teacher to prepare notes in advance of class and project them onto the screen for all students to see; and it is unnecessary for the teacher to darken the room or turn her back to the students. In many ways it is the perfect technology for supporting the kind of instruction that takes place in most classrooms today.

In one of the two quotations opening this chapter, Karen Sheingold argues that school restructuring, new forms of learning and teaching, and new technology provide a kind of synergy that can lead to new forms of schooling. I agree. Skeptics will argue that we are merely going through another cycle of reform; school reforms come almost every decade; the schools absorb as many of the new ideas as they want and reject the rest. The result is that schools change very little where it truly counts—in the classroom.

I think the forces driving the Information Age are irresistible. It is impossible both to participate fully in the culture and yet resist its defining features. Thus, if the schools are an "immovable object" (and I don't believe they are), they are beginning to meet the "irresistible force"—Information Age technology.

The analogy I carry in my head is that of a volcano erupting in Hawaii, spewing forth ash and lava. We have all seen pictures of such eruptions and what follows. The lava slowly oozes its way down the mountain toward the sea. No device or structure raised by human beings can block it. It either consumes all obstacles in fire or rolls over them. Finally, the lava reaches the sea—nature's immovable object. Throughout the process there is a lot of noise, smoke and steam that can distract one's attention from the fundamental process that is occurring: The landscape is being transformed. In the most dramatic cases, entirely new islands appear. A volcanic eruption changes the environment in unpredictable ways; it is also irresistible.

Information Age technology is like that volcano. It is changing the landscape of American culture in ways we either take for granted or scarcely notice. There are holdouts. Many of us resist placing telephones in our cars or buying mobile telephones; to date we see no need for them. Some believe that television is a corrupting influence, and will not have it in their homes. I know such people; I am largely sympathetic to their views. But most people who think television can be corrosive buy one anyway and try to control its use.

I cannot predict how schools will accommodate to the force of computers and other electronic technology. Some schools will move more quickly than others; some teachers will not change at all. The process may be slow enough that many teachers will retire before they are forced to change. Some will quit teaching, and it is likely that some will remain anachronisms in a greatly altered school environment—a kind of antique surrounded by modernity, refusing even to use the telephones that have been installed in their classrooms.

But schools will change! I don't know whether teachers will use the technology in the ways constructivists anticipate; reformers have urged teachers to adopt similar progressive ideas in the past with mostly negative results. Perhaps technology will support constructivist approaches and make learner-centered instruction a practice as well as a theory this time. I don't know whether schools will have site-based management or some other kind of organizational structure. Other theories of learning and school organization will appear. The exact shape of future schools is unclear. But of this I am certain: Schools will be unable to resist the new technology. The new technology will be used in schools because the schools have no reasonable defense for rejecting it.

I don't know what people thought of the pony express during the brief time it was depended upon to deliver mail to remote regions. Today it is treated as a romantic part of the past. The pony express gave way to the telegraph and to railroads not because the ponies slowed down or the riders grew careless. Try as they might, they could not transmit messages as rapidly as the telegraph. People were mainly interested in sending messages, not supporting the pony express.

Technology will be used in schools because it appeals to students and may enhance learning. The use of technology will have a profound effect on schools. It challenges the very relationship between students and teachers, because technology enables learners to gain control of their own learning. In the past, schools have been places where people in authority decided what would be taught (and possibly learned), at what age, and in what sequence. They have also decided what will not be taught—what is not *approved knowledge*. The new technology provides access to information that was once under the control of teachers.

Years ago, as a high school teacher, I received a note from a colleague who was teaching a course in American history for the first time. He had assigned students reading assignments from one set of books while he turned to other books as sources for his lectures. The note said, "The game is up. The students know where I am getting my information." That is what is happening today. "The game is up." No teacher can compete with the power and the capability of the new technology, so long as the teacher's role is defined strictly as presenter of information. If teachers and schools try to sustain that role, they will be whipped. On the other hand, no teachers will be replaced by a machine unless they attempt to do only what the machine can do better.

Within schools, football coaches are often the leading users of technology. Coaches have made films or videotapes of games—even practices—for years. They use the videotapes to teach the players where further skill improvements are required, to analyze opponent weaknesses, and to develop strategies for the next game. Videotapes are viewed as indispensable by coaches; yet no one, least of all coaches, believes that videotape has eliminated the need for coaches.

It may be that the technology will be first used most extensively by privately-financed schools, such as Sylvan Learning Systems, Kaplan Educational Centers, or equivalents of the Edison Schools. Privately financed, successful schools demonstrating the value of technology may provide the incentive to persuade public institutions of the instructional value of technology.

Perhaps public schools employing technology in restructured environments will begin as magnet or even charter schools; if they have success, then technology may spread to the remainder of the schools in a district. Possibly the technological challenge to public education will come from home schooling, when parents discover that through technology they not only retain current home schooling advantages but also gain access to the academic resources of the public schools.

The genie is out of the bottle. It is no longer necessary to learn about the American War of Independence by sitting in Mrs. Smith's classroom and hearing her version of it. There are more powerful and efficient ways to learn about the Revolutionary War, and they are all potentially under the control of the learner. Schools will either come to terms with this fact, or they will be ignored.

It is not going to be easy for schools to change. The current reform effort has been compared to changing a tire on a car while continuing to speed down the highway. The job is much harder than that, because it is not repair but transformation that is required. It is more akin to changing a car into an airplane while continuing to drive the car. We are asking schools to become something different, without a clear picture of what the new institution is, while continuing to satisfy the public that the old purposes of schooling are being served as well as or better than in the past.

It is much easier to reengineer a business firm. What does a firm do if it wants to drop a product or stop a service? It can close the old plant and lay off the workers. If it wants to produce a new product or start a new service, it may buy a firm that is already doing what it wants to do or hire people who are experts in the new product or service.

What can a school board do? It can employ a new superintendent who promotes the new ideas and may remain in the position long enough to see them fully implemented. It cannot lay off existing teachers and replace them with new ones. It can provide incentives for existing teachers, offer training in the new techniques, and give moral support. But teachers have many ways to stiff-arm suggestions from superintendents and board members. For one thing, they can close their classroom doors and teach as they always have. Furthermore, many in the community will disagree with the direction the board is proposing and try to sabotage the reform. It will not be easy!

Availability and Use of Technology in Schools Today[2]

No one knows for certain what kind of technology exists in schools, how it is used, how much it is used, whether what exists is actually available to teachers, and whether what exists is broken, worn-out, or still in unopened boxes. It is hard enough to maintain an up-to-date inventory within a given school district without trying to do the same for the nation. Various people and organizations have conducted surveys on technology use, and these provide some clues as to what exists generally.

Computers. We know that the number of computers in schools has grown enormously since 1983. At that time it was estimated that there were fewer than 50,000 computers in all schools; by 1994 the estimate was revised to 5.5 million. In 1981 only about 18 percent of schools had one or more computers for instruction; by 1994 this figure had risen to 98 percent. There is hardly a school in America without at least one computer.

These figures tell us very little about student access to computers. In 1985 the median number of computers in K-6 elementary schools that used computers was 3; it rose to about 18 in 1989. In high schools during the same two periods the numbers were 16 and 39. By 1994, the ratio of students to computers across all grades was 14 students per computer. Thus while there has been rapid growth in the number of computers in each school, the opportunity for a typical student to have access to a computer has remained very limited. In 1989 a student might have access to a computer one hour per week or an estimated four percent of all instructional time.

A second issue is where computers are placed and how they are used. The most common pattern in schools is to cluster 20 or so machines in a single laboratory and then schedule classes in the lab once a week. Ten years ago, computers were used mainly to teach programming, to teach about computers (computer literacy), and to run drill and practice exercises. More recently, computers have been used for enrichment and as work tools, and less for purposes of computer literacy. However, in elementary schools computers continue to be used heavily to teach basic skills, and this pattern is growing in high schools. Federal funds for at-risk children have been a major source of school funding for computers, so it is hardly surprising that a major school use is for teaching basic skills and remedial instruction. The use of computers to support instruction in the academic areas or for exploration by students is sharply limited. Many American students have more access to a computer at home than at school.

Most computers are purchased as stand-alone machines. It is possible to connect computers, either locally (local area network or LAN) or at a distance (wide area network or WAN). The advantage of networks is that people can work together and share information across locations. Computer networks are common in business and higher education; the use of networks in schools is growing but still small. School LANs are used mainly to support integrated learning systems (ILS) within a school. Thus far, relatively little has been done to foster communications among classrooms. Schools with modems have access to commercial network services, such as Prodigy, CompuServe, Apple Link or America Online. A rapidly increasing number of schools are beginning to use the Internet, a service originally created by the Department of Defense to connect researchers at labs and universities, and which now connects many kinds of groups world-wide. The Clinton administration wishes to build a national electronic infra-structure that would increase opportunities for schools to be connected to outside resources.

Video. Video use in schools seems to be growing and taking different forms than in the past. Instructional television, in which a program is broad-cast to schools at scheduled times during the school day from a state-oper-ated or district-run studio, continues to exist, but it does not seem so signifi-cant as before. Many of these programs were developed nationally through a consortium led by the Agency for Instructional Technology. The programs were designed to fit the school curriculum as determined by the state departments of education that were the most prominent consortium members.

As a result of federal financing through the Star Schools program, many schools are able to use courses delivered by satellite broadcast nationally and originating from a single source at a predetermined time. These pro-grams typically feature courses that are difficult for small schools to offer on their own, e.g., courses in German or Japanese language and advanced courses in mathematics and the sciences. Rural schools in particular have taken advantage of these offerings; about one-third of all rural schools have the capability to receive satellite broadcasts.

Commercial sources also provide programming to schools. In 1994 Whittle Communications, Inc., reportedly offered its programs to more than 12,000 schools reaching 8 million students. The principal program was a 10-minute news show called *Channel One*. The program and all of the equipment provided the schools were paid for with two minutes of adver-tising that accompanied each show. CNN has a rival news program called *CNN Newsroom*. This 15-minute news show is broadcast early in the morn-ing over the regular CNN cable channel. Schools are permitted to tape the program and use it as they please.

The Corporation for Public Broadcasting is developing new programming for schools, and the Learning Channel and the Discovery Channel both pro-vide programs that offer useful information for schools.

As a result of this programming, the VCR has become one of the most ubiquitous pieces of school technology. Virtually every school in the United States has at least one; in certain subject areas teachers have been collect-ing tapes they can use with their classes. The videotape has taken the place of film for instruction.

CD-ROM and videodiscs offer other ways for schools to employ video. Today, their use, while still limited, is growing rapidly. According to Quality Education Data Inc. 26 percent of all school districts had videodisc technology in 1994 as compared to 18 percent in 1992-93.

Results. It would be wonderful if we could point to specific data that would demonstrate conclusively that the use of one technology or another produced better results than some other technology or approach. Alas, as was pointed out in Chapter 3, the problem is not so simple.

First of all, the existence of a particular technology does not prescribe how it will be used. One English teacher might use computers mainly for drill and practice on grammar and spelling while another English teacher is allowing students to use the computers for word processing. One teacher may be using a videotape to spark interest preliminary to a month-long study; a second teacher may be using a videotape because she has nothing else prepared for class on that day. *Channel One* has been shown to increase students' knowledge of geography and world affairs when the program is actively used by teachers; but when it is ignored by both teachers and students, little learning occurs. *How* the technology is used is critically important.

Much of the evaluation research on media use is based upon a specific intervention and focuses on short-term results: Did the students receiving instruction by means of computer-assisted instruction (CAI) perform better on a short-answer examination than did the control group, who were denied the CAI treatment? In studies of this kind, the experimental group nearly always wins, but seldom does the investigator study the two groups a year or two later to find out if the gain survives. Much of the data on ILS systems are of this kind. The studies are interesting, but of marginal value to policy makers.[3]

What we need are studies of a different order. When students and teachers are immersed in technology *over time,* will we detect changes in how students learn and teachers teach? While it may be important to see some gain on a particular test, those who are trying to reform schools have larger goals in mind. Before we spend billions of dollars to equip every student with a computer at home and one at school, and before we spend millions to equip teachers and to provide them with the necessary training, we need to know if such a colossal investment of public funds makes sense. We cannot be certain, but the study reported below should encourage us.

One Suggestive Experiment. In 1986, Apple Computer, Inc. launched a project called *Apple Classrooms of Tomorrow (ACOT).*[4] They began with seven classrooms representing what they hoped was a cross section of K-12 schools. They gave each participating student and teacher two computers: one for the home and one for the school. The goal of the project was to see how routine use of the computer (as contrasted to one hour per week in a lab, for example) would affect how students learn and how teachers teach.

One issue the project hoped to confront was any negative effects that prolonged exposure to computers might have. Some critics have worried that students using computers extensively would become less social or "brain dead" from looking at the computer screen all day. At the end of two years, the investigators learned that some of their worst fears were groundless, namely:

1. Teachers were not hopelessly illiterate with technology. They could use computers to accomplish their work.

2. Children did not become social isolates. ACOT classes showed more evidence of spontaneous, cooperative learning than did traditional classes.

3. Children did not become bored by the technology over time. Instead their desire to use it for their purposes increased with use.

4. Children, even very young children, had no problem becoming adept at the keyboard. With very little training, second- and third-grade children were soon typing 25-30 words per minute with 95 percent accuracy, more than twice as fast as children that age can usually write.

5. Software was not a problem. Teachers found programs—including productivity tools—to employ in their classes.

Standardized test scores showed that students were doing as well as they might have been expected to perform without the computers; some were performing better. The studies showed that ACOT students wrote better and were able to complete units of study more rapidly. In one case, students finished the year's study of mathematics by the beginning of April. In short, productivity did not suffer and in some cases improved.

What I found most interesting, however, was that classroom observers noticed differences in the behavior of teachers and students. Students were taking more responsibility for their own learning, and teachers were working more as mentors and less like presenters.

By the end of the fourth year, classrooms were different than when they had begun; teachers were teaching differently, although they did not all teach alike. Each teacher seemed to have adjusted his/her own style to the computer-rich environment, but all of the teachers were aware of the changes that had occurred in their own professional outlook.

The students also had changed, especially the ACOT students at West High School, a school serving urban, blue-collar families in Columbus, Ohio. Twenty-one freshmen were selected at random from the student body to participate in the study. They stayed with the program all four years, until their graduation. All 21 graduated, whereas the study body as a whole had a 30 percent dropout rate. Ninety percent went on to college, while only 15 percent of non-ACOT students sought higher education; seven of the ACOT students were offered full college scholarships and several businesses offered to hire those who did not intend to go to college. ACOT students had half the absentee rate, and they had accumulated more than their share of academic honors. But perhaps the most important finding was the difference exhibited by these students in how they did their work. They routinely, without prompting, employed inquiry, collaborative, technological, and problem-solving skills of the kind promoted by the school reform movement.

This is only one study; it is unwise to depend too greatly upon its findings. But those who believe that technology is the key to school reform and more powerful learning by students can take hope from this investigation.

They may also be encouraged by the results of a 1994 study commissioned by the Software Publishers Association and conducted by an independent technology consulting firm, Interactive Educational Systems Design, Inc.[5] The study reviewed research on educational technology conducted from 1990 through 1994. The report was based upon 133 research reviews and reports on original research projects. Some of the conclusions of that study were:

- Educational technology has a significant positive effect on achievement in all subject areas, across all levels of school and in regular classrooms as well as those for special-needs students;

- Educational technology has positive effects on student attitudes;

- The degree of effectiveness is influenced by the student population, the instructional design, the teacher's role, how students are grouped, and the levels of student access to technology;

- Technology makes instruction more student-centered, encourages cooperative learning, and stimulates increased teacher/student interaction;

- Positive changes in the learning environment evolve over time and do not occur quickly.

These conclusions are largely consistent with the ACOT study. While the study was commissioned by an organization that has a stake in the results, the conclusions seem consistent with other research findings.

The Future of Technology in Schools

Thus far we have focused on technology available to schools today. But what of the future? We are only at the beginning of the Information Age. Tools we now treat as technical marvels will seem primitive in five years. Commodore Pets, IBM Pcjrs., and the first Apple machines are throwaway items today. We can predict that technology will become more powerful, faster, cheaper, and easier to use. We can also predict that new devices that we can scarcely imagine today will be in the market before the end of the decade. Schools that expect to invest in a single computer system and then forget technology purchases for several years will be surprised and disappointed. Schools must make decisions regarding additions and/or upgrades to their technology every year, in line with their own strategic plans.

In this section we will examine three, familiar technologies that are likely to affect schools over the next five years. None of the examples provided is unrealistic; all either already exist or plans for their development are in place. The fact that most schools may not be using these tools today is not the issue; they could be using them now for instructional purposes, if they wished to do so. The section closes with three interpretations of how technology is likely to develop in the future and the impact of these developments on schools.

Three Examples of Technology Schools Will Use

While I cannot possibly treat all of the various technologies available to the schools, I have chosen three that seem likely to have the greatest impact. We start with the oldest of these technologies, one that has been available for many years in every business office and nearly every home, but one only now reaching the classroom—the telephone.

Telephone. In the past, it was not deemed necessary for teachers to have telephones; it was thought that teachers would merely waste time by talking on the phone when they should be teaching; now it is difficult to see how teachers can do their work without them.

One use of the telephone is to communicate with parents and students. In order to avoid class interruptions, schools have voice mail capabilities, so that parents can leave messages for teachers throughout the day, and teachers can return calls when they have time. The service also makes it possible for teachers to leave recorded messages for parents or students about homework, forthcoming parent/teacher events, etc. Teachers can communicate with parents individually or as a group.

The telephone is also the primary bridge to distance learning. Students who are forced for health or other reasons to remain at home can partici-

"FOR FURTHER INFORMATION, DIAL
1-800 I-DO-MATH."

pate in class through the speaker phone. By adding audiographics software and hardware, teachers and students can also communicate by means of graphic images. The teacher can send pictures and graphics to students while she is speaking; she can also use an electronic tablet much as she would a blackboard at school.

It is also possible to add video to the telephone connection. Teachers can teach students who are in a classroom at another location. Using video conference technology, the teacher can see her class at the same time the students are watching her. Like a conference telephone call, the signal can go to more than one location at a time, thereby allowing the teacher to instruct as many as eight classes simultaneously. Schools that are most likely to use this technology are schools that want to offer specialized courses— e.g., Japanese language, advanced calculus—but do not have access to a properly qualified teacher. By means of interactive distance learning, one teacher can be shared with several classrooms at the same time.

Video teleconferencing can also be used to bring resources to the school that would not otherwise be available. Students can interview their congressmen, other public officials, and business leaders by telephone. Teachers are also able to use teleconferencing for professional purposes, including consulting with other teachers and taking further college courses.

Computers. Computers will continue to become faster, more powerful, easier to use, smaller, and cheaper. They will be connected to LANs within a building and school districts and connected through WANs to the world. In addition to computers that sit on desks, students will have their own portable computers, about the size of a notebook, that they can carry with them. Computers in the near future will be capable of handling voice, data, and video. They will be able to operate by wireless communication, and be docked into a network.

Computers will be easier to use. They will come with keyboards, but they will also respond to voice commands, gestures, and touch screens. Students will be able to take notes on their computer; it will recognize their handwriting and convert their script digitally so that it can be stored or printed in typed characters.

Whiteboards will either replace or complement chalkboards in class-rooms. Whiteboards are thin, panel display units capable of accepting video and data inputs. Both teachers and students will be able to project their ideas to the whiteboard from their computers as they discuss their ideas.

New computers will be driven by industry standards so that the prod-ucts of various computers can be linked together. They will be more durable, and less prone to breakdown. As the cost goes down, they will also be more readily discarded after several years of use.

The market for software will grow, eventually surpassing textbook sales. This will bring many large companies as well as small software firms into the market, thereby assuring higher quality software and lower prices.

Teachers will be less dependent upon commercial software than they are today. Without bothering to learn arcane computer languages, they will be able to add to or even modify commercial software, adding their own ideas to the instructional program. The teacher will become less a cook of prepackaged food and more a chef.

Teachers will store their teaching materials electronically. Rather than rummaging through closets and boxes, they will find their units and visuals in data storage, waiting to be presented. Both teachers and students will have access to servers with enormous storage capacity. When a teacher begins a new unit, she will be able to draw upon a wide range of materials she can use in class.

Teachers will have access to resources that were previously unavailable to them. Expert systems, designed to respond to problems confronting classroom teachers, will help teachers diagnose children with reading or math problems, or children who are hyperactive. The programs will analyze the problems and offer solutions, operating somewhat like medical diagnosis systems work today. Teachers will be able to tap into databases that are contributed by other teachers. Many teachers already have access to the ERIC system for research reports; these resources will grow further and become easier to use. Teachers also will have access to test banks, featuring a wide variety of assessments that can be employed for evaluating students.

Much of the job of seeking out these and other resources will be done by the computer itself. Teachers will have "personal electronic assistants," whose job is to seek answers to questions teachers have and reproduce the answers in a convenient form.

Video. Schools have had access to video for four decades. In general, educational programming has been delivered in a broadcast mode over public channels operated by the state or community or by for-profit or not-for-profit consortia. In recent years, the cable industry has opened new sources of educational programming; the local cable supplier brings the cable to the school; national content providers such as CNN, Arts & Entertainment, and Discovery channels provide programming. Schools can either use the program when it arrives or record it on videotape for later use.

More recently, new enterprises have begun to compete for the school video market. Whittle Communications, Inc., may have been the first. To gain access to schools, Whittle provided video receivers for each classroom, wired each school building, provided one VCR for each school and free programming in exchange for the schools requiring all students to watch *Channel One*.

New commercial video efforts are underway. Galaxy Classroom beams science and language arts programs to elementary schools in 21 states and Mexico. Galaxy employs a 10-pound, 19-inch digital broadcast disk, monitors, dedicated fax lines, and electronic mail to deliver its lessons. Students are encouraged to fax messages about the show to Galaxy producers, asking questions and offering program suggestions, many of which are shared in later broadcasts.

The telephone companies have also entered the video market. In Indiana, for example, Ameritech is offering a new program called *Vision Athena*. Ameritech does not provide programming; in this way it is like the local cable provider. But Ameritech is providing fiber-optic capability to all of the Indiana schools in its service area, and contributing a basic equipment package to each school, together with a subsidy for wiring the school and for planning how to use the new capability. Ameritech believes that schools will create their own programs or buy programs from service providers, such as universities, museums, and zoos.

For several years, textbook publishers have been offering videodiscs, videotapes, or CD-ROMs to accompany their print materials. In 1994 Scholastic, Inc., began an elementary school science program to accompany its *Super Science Red* program, which appears as a regular journal for elementary schools. This program is being tested in Georgia with partial support from the Georgia Educational Television System; Scholastic and the State of Georgia intend to market the program nationally.

In the near future, teachers will have access to a tremendous variety of video resources. Some of the products will be stored on large video servers and can be called into use on demand from cable or telephone companies. Other resources will be provided live by cable companies, tele-phone companies, or other enterprises. These firms will compete in the market on quality and price. Finally, teachers will be able to use video for gaining access to professional development via distance-learning technology.

Three Perspectives

What can we conclude from these developments? What does the future hold for schools?

Integration, Interaction, and Intelligence. Telephone, computer, and video were all treated above as if they were likely to continue as sepa-rate enterprises. In fact, we can expect an *integration* of these technologies. Voice, data, and images will be brought together into one package. One current example is desktop video. In a single, relatively inexpensive unit one has the capabilities of a telephone (voice), computer (data storage and manipulation), and video (sending and receiving moving images). Those who use the machine can talk to people at a distance, exchange documents and work collaboratively, while seeing the other person.

Technology will also become more *interactive*. In the field of distance learning rather than one-way video and two-way audio communication, teachers and students will see each other simultaneously, thereby making distance learning more like face-to-face classroom teaching. Computer-based instruction will also be designed to respond more to the learners' interests and abilities, giving them greater control over what they need to learn and the pace at which they wish to learn it. And computer searches, which can now be bewildering to the casual user, will become easier to use and more responsive to what the user needs rather than exhibiting every-thing that might be available. Greater interactivity will make instructional programs even more powerful than they are today.

Finally, technology will have greater *intelligence*. This intelligence will be displayed in several ways. First of all, the technology will have more features and greater capacity. Second, it will have the capability to learn from the user so that it can customize its services to fit the user's learning style and interests. Future technology will provide not only databases but knowledge bases. And the technology will be able to stay abreast of that information most valued by the user and alert her to its availability.

Integration, interaction, and intelligence: These are three features we can expect of technology in the future. They will change the way technology is employed in schools.

From Classroom to Just-in-Time Learning. Alan Chute, director of the Center for Excellence in Distance Learning for AT&T, believes that those engaged in corporate education are likely to migrate across three

Figure 1. Instructional Technology Model

Stage III Just-In-Time Performance Support	•Artificial intelligence •Knowledge systems •Hypermedia •Hypertext •Videodisc teletraining •CBT teletraining •Computer based training (CBT)
Stage II Distance Learning	•Video teletraining •Audiographic teletraining •Audio teletraining •Videodisc •Electronic mail •Computer graphics •Voice mail •Computer •Video
Stage I Classroom Learning	•Print •Graphics

stages of technology use. (See Figure 1) Stage 1 is a traditional classroom. The instruction occurs at the same time and the same place, with both the teacher and student present. The technologies that are most appropriate for stage 1 learning are computers, print, videotapes, and graphics. Increasingly, corporations are turning to distance-learning technologies to save time and money. In traditional distance learning, the teacher and the students are in different places but meeting at the same time. The technology appropriate for distance learning includes audio teleconferencing, audio-graphics, and interactive video teleconferencing. The third stage is called *Just-In-Time Performance Support* (JITPS). This assumes the instructor and the learner are at different places and working at different times. In this mode of learning, the learner obtains the information he needs when he wants it at whatever location he may be: office, car, hotel, or home. The information he receives is no less and no more than he needs for the task at hand. Chute believes that hypermedia, knowledge systems, and artificial intelligence are needed for this stage of activity.

Chute's scheme is based upon his experience with adult learners in American corporations. It is not clear that the same migration will take place in schooling. However, his ideas fit easily with the delivery of profes-sional education for teachers. In-service education may no longer be delivered in face-to-face encounters with college faculty but come by means of distance learning or JITPS technology.

Relationship of Technology to School Reform. According to Barbara Means, "The primary motivation for using technologies in education is the belief that they will support superior forms of learning."[6] Whether this will prove to be true or not is uncertain, but she and her colleagues have developed a chart that relates technology to education reform features. (See Figure 2) The features include those she believes should be emphasized because they support "learner-centered" instruction. While it is true that the examples of technology cited could be used for other purposes as well, her examples seem especially well matched to each aspect of reform.

University Role in Applications of Technology in Education

Most of the energy and ideas for technology applications in schools have come from private enterprise: Apple, IBM, Jostens Learning, CCC, MECC, and TERC. Universities are distinguished more by their absence than by their presence in this aspect of school reform.

In the past, school reform was supported by university-based research and development programs. I noted in Chapter 2 that most of the BU reformers had university bases. But universities as a whole have demonstrated little interest in the application of technology in K-12 schools. There are notable exceptions. One is the Institute for the Learning Sciences, established at Northwestern University in 1989 and directed by Roger C. Shank. The goal of the institute is to create innovative, computer-based learning environments, based on leading-edge research in cognitive science and artificial intelligence. The institute attempts to be a catalyst for change in school systems by developing software that alters how and what children learn.

For many years, Bank Street College of Education hosted the U.S. Department of Education Center for Technology in Education, directed by Karen Sheingold. While Sheingold was at Bank Street College the center conducted studies of the ways technology was employed in schools. The center has since moved from Bank Street College.

In Chapter 3, I referred to the work of John Bransford and his colleagues at Vanderbilt University. Their focus has been primarily on the development of video and computer-based products that provide authentic settings for student learning with emphasis on research and development of products that affect learning.

Many schools and colleges of education provide computer literacy courses for teachers-in-training, and a few have established alliances with schools

Figure 2.

Features of Education Reform and Supportive Technologies[7]

Features of Education Reform							Potentially Supportive Technology
Heterogeneous Groupings	Performance-Based Assessment	Authentic and Multi-disciplinary Tasks	Collaborative Work	Interactive Modes of Instruction	Student Exploration	Teacher as Facilitator	Given a supportive instructional setting, the following technologies can support various features of reform, as indicated in this chart. It is possible to use the technologies in ways that promote other aspects of reform and many other exemplary products are currently available.
	•	•			•	•	**Electronic Databases**
	•				•		**Electronic Reference Tools**
•	•	•	•	•	•	•	**Hypermedia**
			•			•	**Intelligent Computer-Assisted Instruction (ICAI)**
				•	•	•	**Intelligent Tools**
	•	•			•	•	**Microcomputer-Based Labs**
	•	•	•	•	•	•	**Microworlds and Simulations**
•	•	•	•		•	•	**Multimedia Tools and Approaches**
•	•	•	•	•	•	•	**Networks and Related Applications**
•				•		•	**Two-way Video/Two-way Audio Distance Learning**
•	•	•	•		•	•	**Videocameras, VCRs, Editors**
	•	•	•	•	•	•	**Videodisc and CD-ROM**
	•	•	•		•	•	**Word Processors/Intelligent Writing Tools**

to test computer-based programs and to support the professional education of teachers.

There is an important role for universities in the field of technology and education. Currently too little is done to link technology with improved methods of teaching and learning: Educational software has not yet achieved the level of quality that is required; teachers are not being adequately trained to use technology effectively, leaving it to the schools to provide basic technology training to new employees; and schools must turn to vendors for advice on what technology they need. There is an important job to be done by universities, and most have not yet accepted the challenge.

Indiana University

One exception is a major effort underway at Indiana University in Bloomington, Indiana. This effort began in 1982 when I was dean of the School of Education. Like many other Schools of Education across the country, our school had gone through a long period of steep retrenchment, cutting budget, faculty, and staff in an attempt to keep pace with declining enrollments. While this was difficult enough, we also were aware that the school was lagging behind changes occurring in schools. For example, I often heard complaints from school superintendents who were having trouble finding teachers with adequate computer knowledge. Some K-12 schools were ahead of our own faculty in the application of technology for instruction. If this were to continue, our reputation would surely suffer.

The School of Education faculty needed to employ technology in their own instruction. The faculty did not use technology largely because it was not available to them, and they were not trained in its use.

With the support of university officials, we launched a major fund-raising campaign aimed at constructing a new building that could serve as a showcase for the use of technology in education. We believed that such a building would inspire faculty to use technology in their own instruction and fill the need to properly prepare teachers. The building could also serve as a magnet for support of research and development on the use of technology in education.

The funding campaign was eventually successful. Approximately $30 million was raised from the federal and Indiana governments, from the private sector, especially AT&T, and from the university. The funds were used to build a new building to house the School of Education, the Education Library, and a new research and development center called the Center for Excellence in Education. Funds were also used to equip the facility to a degree that it could serve as a model site for people who wish to learn about system architecture for technology and application tools. Additional funds were provided to train faculty and staff and support research and the development of new courses.

The Wendell W. Wright Education Building. In 1992 the Indiana University School of Education began the fall semester in a new, state-of-the-art facility designed to support professional education with all of the latest tools of the Information Age. The facility is served by AT&T's SYSTI-MAX Premises Distribution System, an integrated, networked, comprehensive cabling system that handles all communications—voice, video, and data—within the building as well as between the building and other distant locations. The communications infrastructure employs single and multimode fiber-optic cable and unshielded twisted-pair copper cable that connect all of the electronic devices. The wiring system supports classrooms, conference rooms, computer labs, offices, and electronic information kiosks. Each classroom is equipped to receive and send video, data, and voice; each office is equipped with computers to connect the faculty to data sources within the building, across the campus, and beyond; each telephone provides multiple capabilities, including voice mail which can be accessed from anywhere.

A unique capability is a video distribution system that can carry up to 60 channels of video throughout the building. Some channels are dedicated and are accessible to only limited use (e.g., counseling psychology faculty who wish to observe clinical sessions remotely from their offices); other channels carry programs throughout the building and are accessible to anyone (e.g., CNN news or a special program in professional education). Faculty can originate video programs from any information outlet found in all of the offices and classrooms, using a variety of delivery modes ranging from compressed digital signals over telephone lines to full-motion video carried by dedicated fiber or by satellite transmission.

The School of Education provides computer classrooms for teacher training on both Apple Macintosh and personal computers; a computer lab is available to students throughout the day, evenings, and weekends; the Education Library has 64 desktop computers and each of the study carrels permits students to plug portable computers into the building's communication system; a high-end computer support lab provides special equipment for faculty and students to create instructional products; electronic kiosks provide information to visitors about the location of offices and services within the building and about the campus as a whole; they are also used to exhibit CD-ROMs and other products developed by faculty and students.

Education faculty, staff, and students are supported by the Office of Education Technology Services (ETS). In 1994, ETS had 10 full-time-equivalent staff and four part-time, graduate student employees. One staff member is required full time to maintain telephone services; a second is needed to maintain and repair computer equipment; a third supports the faculty in their use of video; a fourth provides training for faculty and staff on the use of new software applications. Some bear overall responsibility for technology planning and for overseeing equipment and software purchases, and others support faculty in their classroom uses of multimedia or in the delivery of distance learning courses by means of interactive video. ETS exists to make certain that no faculty member is discouraged from using technology because of lack of experience; it also serves to inspire and lead faculty to experiment with technology applications that were previously unknown to them.

The IU School of Education quickly recognized that obtaining equipment and a state-of-the-art facility would not by itself yield desirable results without an adequate support system. Thus, the School of Education invests substantial amounts of its operating budget into providing support services to faculty and staff in order to make their work as easy as possible.

The results of these investments are programs that were inconceivable to IU's Education faculty in the past. Faculty deliver graduate courses into Indiana schools using interactive video; they bring guest lecturers into their classrooms by means of live video projection; they are connected to their students by means of electronic conferences; they conduct faculty business across multiple campus sites by both video and audio conferencing; and they connect schools throughout the world electronically to on-going research and development projects. The administration of the School of Education is increasingly paperless: Most communication occurs and records are maintained electronically. Increasingly, students are expected to sustain electronic communication with their peers and instructors.

Faculty from other Indiana University colleges and departments schedule special events in the Wright Building so as to take advantage of technology resources that are not generally available throughout the university. The School of Education is now perceived to have the best facilities for teaching on the Bloomington campus, a decided change from the past.

Center for Excellence in Education (CEE). One result of the major fundraising effort was the establishment of a new Indiana University research and development center devoted to exploring appropriate applications of technology in education. Since its formal launch in 1992, CEE has focused on four areas: demonstration of technology applications in education, research and development of new educational applications, training, and technology planning.

Demonstration. Educators want to observe how technology can be used to enhance instruction when there are adequate resources to support it. During its first year CEE hosted nearly 250 delegations and a total of more than 3,000 people who traveled to Bloomington from all over the world. Some were interested in particular building features: how the building distributes video, using a combination of fiber and twisted-copper pair wire;

others were interested in the use of video teleconferencing for distance learning, and so on. Perhaps 50 percent of the visitors represented elementary and secondary schools; the remaining half were nearly equally divided between representatives from corporations and from higher education.

Since the first year, the majority of visits have been for one or two days. CEE staff confer with the visitors before they come so that the visitors can accomplish exactly what they want to do. In 1994 visitors included: Indiana public schools such as Tri-North Middle School and Brown County Schools; community colleges such as Florida Community College in Jacksonville, Florida and Kellogg Community College in Battle Creek, Michigan; universities such as the University of Kentucky College of Education and Illinois Wesleyan University; government agencies such as the Internal Revenue Service; and corporations such as Lucky Gold Star from Korea and Hughes Training, Inc.

Schools need places to go where they can receive vendor-neutral, client-centered advice. CEE seeks to serve clients by assembling all of the resources available at Indiana University and beyond to address visitors' needs.

Research and Development. CEE has supported a wide variety of research and development projects. Some were aimed at helping School of Education faculty redesign their courses to take advantage of new technology; others have been directed at helping School of Education faculty apply distance-learning technology to the continuing professional education of teachers. The experiments have not been limited to School of Education faculty. Music School, Business School, Medical School, and Telecommunications faculty have also pursued R & D projects with CEE support. Some projects have involved direct support to Indiana schools. One experiment conducted during 1993/94 involved the use of audio-graphic distance-learning systems in a dozen schools. CEE provided the equipment and technical support, while the schools provided the teachers, the students, and paid for communication charges.

In 1994 the two largest projects underway were the Virtual Textbook and the World School for Adventure Learning. The Virtual Textbook (VT) anticipates a time when the printed textbook no longer provides the organizing core of the curriculum, having been replaced by information that is open, rather than prepackaged, and subject to learner control. The VT is a small notebook-size computer capable of sending and receiving voice, data, and video. It operates in both a wireless and connected mode. It has a keyboard but can be operated by both voice and pen commands. We expect that every student will eventually have one; while they will be used in school, because they are portable, they can also be carried home for work.

CEE's interest is not so much in engineering the hardware but in developing the standards that will control the operation of such machines and in creating examples of the instructional software that will run on them. CEE staff believe that many public and private organizations will develop modules of information suitable for use in classrooms that can operate on these computers. Their job is to determine how to make these modules easily accessible and affordable for schools to use. CEE is working with several corporations in the design and development of this product.

The World School for Adventure Learning is testing the notion of linking students worldwide with exciting current adventures. Initial work was done in collaboration with Hamline University, the University of St. Thomas in St. Paul, Minnesota, and the University of Michigan. These universities are linked to the International Arctic Project, an effort by five professional explorers to cross the Arctic Ocean by dogsled and canoe, and nearly 100 schools around the world participate in the project. The teachers who are part of the project share curriculum ideas with each other, using the Internet for communication. In addition to communicating with the Arctic explorers, the students also undertake adventures in their own communities, e.g., reclaiming a contaminated lake, and share their adventures with other schools.

In 1994 CEE collaborated with Turner Educational Services in the development of electronic field trips. Just as schools have often planned field trips for students so that they can actually see firsthand what is occurring, CEE anticipates a time when many electronic field trips will be underway during a school year and students can participate in many of them. The first field trip, in May 1994, involved a visit to the Civil War battlefield in Gettysburg, Pennsylvania. Students from all over the United States were able to watch while students were taken on a tour of the battlefield; they saw reenactments of the battle and were able to phone in questions to people on site. Just as with other, well-planned field trips, there were activities for students to carry out before and after the field trip. These activities included accessing databases that contained additional materials about the battle and those who participated in it.

In the future, schools will have the opportunity to visit places throughout the earth and in outer space, using telecommunications technology. CEE is exploring how schools can gain maximum pedagogical value from such trips.

Training. While CEE is not established to offer academic courses, it does provide short-term training for clients. CEE tries to fill gaps that academic departments or other organizations are unable to satisfy. For example, during the past two years there has been considerable interest in the use of two-way, interactive video (either full-motion or compressed digital video signals) for purposes of distance learning. These technologies are used most frequently in corporate settings, but interest in their use has grown in higher education and K-12 schools. A primary problem is how to exploit these tools pedagogically. To resolve this problem, CEE offers short (two-day) and week-long (usually summer only) sessions to provide hands-on tutoring in the use of distance-learning technologies. Because many teachers have discovered the Internet as a source of instructional materials, CEE has also conducted workshops for teachers, librarians, and administrators on ways to use the Internet efficiently.

Technology Planning. This area of interest grew out of visitors' needs for advice on which computers they should purchase. Some teachers and school administrators asked for purchase advice before they had a clear idea of how the equipment would advance their curriculum goals or their vision for their school. Many schools, as well as universities, have not thought about the relationship of technology to other purposes and needs they have. They have assumed the first step was to decide what equipment to buy; later they could decide how to use it. Much money has been wasted because schools have not fully considered the kind of learning they wish to support, and the roles they expect teachers to play in the future.

As a result of this experience, CEE offers Strategic Planning Seminars that bring school-based technology planning teams to CEE for a total of six days, spread over the entire academic year. Each team represents a larger planning team in its home district. The sessions in Bloomington are conducted as seminars, in which the teams address questions that are important to them. Participants typically deal with many school reform issues, ranging from curriculum matters to changing roles for teachers. Technology questions are blended with questions about the reform of schooling and the kind of instructional environment each school is trying to create. The various school teams learn from each other and encourage risk-taking beyond what they might have been willing to accept on their own. The result of each seminar is a strategic plan, written by the respective school teams and designed with their own schools in mind, but based upon interactions with many others who have considered the same issues. In addition to these seminars, CEE consults with architects, contractors, school boards, and administrators on issues relating to electronic infrastructure for school buildings and equipment requirements.

What is taking place at Indiana University, within the School of Education and the Center for Excellence in Education, is not the only way that universities might contribute to school reform by means of technology. The effort nationally to build effective use of technology in schools will require other universities in the nation to acquire and focus resources for this purpose.

Conclusion

Karen Sheingold is correct; it is not likely that we will get school reform or higher-level learning by students without success with technology. The new technology makes it possible to provide the resources students require to take charge of their learning; the technology invites teachers to assume new roles. There is simply no way for a teacher to compete as a "fountain of information" when she is compared to the resources available to her students.

Will school reform, new approaches to learning, and technology come together and result in the kinds of schools the reformers want? It is too soon to tell. After 15 years and a massive investment of dollars in computers and other technology, relatively few schools are equipped adequately for the job. We continue to prepare teachers who lack the knowledge and skills to use technology fully, and for many years, most instruction will be continued to be provided by teachers who are already employed in schools.

Transforming schools into different kinds of institutions is a massive undertaking, but we cannot lose heart or be impatient. There are reasons to be optimistic, as the next chapter suggests, and there are things we can do now to assist the reform process that the final chapter will address.

One of my colleagues is known to cut through discussions that seem to be going nowhere by the comment: "Are we just going to talk about this or are we going to do something?" Are we just going to talk about new kinds of schools or are we going to create them? Talk is easy, but it often results in little more than policy statements and declarations. Doing something takes time, persistence, and dollars. But it will result in schools that we can all point to with pride.

Chapter 5

TECHNOLOGY REVOLUTION IN SCHOOLS

In times of change, the learners inherit the earth, while the learned find themselves beautifully equipped to deal with a world that no longer exists. Eric Hoffer

Teachers of America, take heart: The revolution has begun. This revolution will change the nature of schooling. Your job will become more challenging and rewarding; you will have more choices. Your students will learn more than under the old regime, and you will be accorded the respect and recognition you deserve as a result of your students' achievements.

I have seen the revolution. I have talked to the revolutionaries, attended their meetings, read their literature, and sat in on their debates. This movement is growing. It has no serious opposition. It will succeed.

What is this revolution? It is the transformation of schooling through the use of technology. It is occurring in classrooms all over the United States. The seeds of the revolution are being planted everywhere, seldom dramatically. Occasionally, there is an announcement that a major grant has been accorded School A that will lead to installing Brand X equipment in all of its schools. But these are the exception. What is occurring nearly every week is that one school board has approved the purchase of ten or 20 computers for use in a school to improve writing skills; another board has approved the high school's use of *Channel One;* still another has set aside funds so that the high school or middle school can subscribe to online, commercial information services, and so on. This revolution is not characterized by a major assault resulting in rapidly sweeping away every custom and practice of the past. This is a slow but steady revolution. Each decision by a school board, act of support by a principal, and initiative by a teacher is changing the nature of schooling.

This revolution is not like any other school reform movement that I have observed, and I have been in the profession for more than 40 years. First of all, it is a grassroots movement. Actions by state and federal governments and by business and industry have helped fuel the revolution, but they did not provide the spark. Teachers and local school administrators are leading this revolution, and they are not leading it in order to save American business or to prove a new theory of learning. They are buying, installing, and using technology simply because they believe students will be less bored and will learn more through the use of the technology than without it. In short, they are using technology to make schools better.

This revolution is eclectic and largely devoid of ideology; therefore, what schools do with the technology varies widely. Much technology is used, especially in elementary grades, for remediation; it provides drill and practice exercises that are boring for teachers to teach; school officials hope the computers will hold kids' attention and save wear and tear on teachers. This approach to learning may irritate the constructivists and many others, but so long as society places an emphasis upon mastering basic skills, we need not be surprised if some schools use technology to meet these goals and to help students pass required tests.

Other schools are using the technology primarily to provide students with productivity tools, such as word processing and spread sheets, to inspire students to make their work more professional in appearance. In other schools, such technology as compressed, interactive video is used to share an instructor across one or more school sites. Technology has its foot in the door of classrooms all across America, and the schools will never be the same.

Some people will be annoyed to learn that there is a revolution underway and they have not been informed or invited to participate. First of all while they may know that millions of dollars have been invested in computers and other technology during the past decade and a half, they have assumed that most teachers have resisted the technology. Secondly, they believe that little has been accomplished by these investments, because there has been no evidence of sharp improvements in SAT and national achievement test scores.

In response to the first point, I agree that many teachers do not yet employ instructional technology and probably will not for some time. The vanguard teachers, as in every revolutionary movement, are the dedicated ones; the rest must be persuaded that the cause is in their interest, and we don't make it easy to convince them. Few schools currently provide computers for each teacher; they must be shared. Teachers are provided little training in how to use the new technology, and seldom is there adequate technical support when the technology breaks down. In such cases, it makes sense for some teachers to continue to do what they are doing rather than spend time learning to use technology.

With regard to the second point, we have considerable evidence that the appropriate use of technology does contribute to student learning. These experimental results, however, are overwhelmed and overlooked when reporting national results. When viewed nationally, despite major investments to date, we have only begun to provide schools what they need. Except in a few cases, students have access to a computer only one hour a week and then for the purpose of working on pre-selected exercises. Imagine the outcry if students had access to a textbook only one day a week or had to share their pencils with 15 other students. Imagine a business, like an insurance company, that had only one computer for each 15 workers who had to take turns entering their data. When access to computers has been sufficient, the results are positive for student learning. This is what the revolutionists know, and what the doubters ignore.

We cannot blame teachers or students if technology has failed to transform all schools. There has not been enough time or enough money for equipment purchase, training, and support. Transforming schooling through technology will work; we have evidence it does. But it will take time, and it will be expensive.

There are also people who do not want the technology revolution to succeed. Some are offended that this reform is truly a grassroots effort. While it is certainly abetted by business and government, it is not a top-down effort, like most educational reforms in this country. This is not a reform hatched in universities or think tanks and handed on to schools to implement. Indeed, universities and most think tanks are largely unconnected to this reform. Obviously, specific professors and researchers are greatly involved, but institutional responses have been erratic: sometimes positive, occasionally negative, usually absent.

Others want to improve schools but do it cheaply. They hope that more regulation, stiffened accountability measures, stirring speeches, coupled with scolding lectures when results do not improve, will do the job. They are wrong, and they are cheapskates.

A few, mainly in universities, are offended by the thought of linking technology to learning. For ideological reasons they wish to keep technology out of schools because it may "de-skill" teachers. Technology may place schools in the service of business and industry; it may exacerbate equity problems. These issues are fundamental to some college professors, but few of the revolutionaries are listening. What may be most threatening to university professors is that they have spent their lives becoming expert in narrow topics, and technology threatens to make their knowledge available to everyone. Much is made of the threat computers pose to K-12 teachers because it challenges their role as keepers and presenters of knowledge. If that threat exists for K-12 teachers, it is even greater for many college professors.

But I have said enough about doubters and skeptics. Let me turn to the revolution itself: Who are the leaders? Where is it taking place? Who supports it? These and other questions deserve answers in order to make the case for the existence of a technology-driven revolution in schooling.

Who are the Revolutionaries?

If you look, you will probably find one in your community, teaching in your neighborhood school. They look like any other teacher. Some are elementary teachers, others are secondary teachers. They represent all of the subject areas, and they have had the same professional training as their colleagues. But they are different.

If I were to try to sketch a profile of a revolutionary teacher I would describe him or her as neither a new teacher nor one about to retire; they have taught long enough to feel comfortable in their jobs and yet be concerned about growing stale. They tend to be independent, self-confident, and unafraid to take risks. They are likely to solve their own problems rather than merely complain about them. Such a revolutionary is Mel Levin.

Mel Levin is *Electronic Learning's* 1994 Educator of the Year.[1] Levin teaches in Prince Hall School, a K-5, inner-city school in Philadelphia. Levin operates a computer lab in the school where he teaches computer skills to all children in grades 1-5, offers computer literacy classes for the parents of Prince Hall School children, and leads a city-wide Technology Users Group for teachers. He was also the driving force behind a school-to-school exchange with Williston-Central School in Vermont, which began with a telecommunications exchange and grew into a face-to-face exchange between the African American students at Prince Hall and the white, largely rural students in Vermont. In 1984 Levin organized the first professional technology conference for elementary and middle school students. The half-day conference, conducted by technology teachers across Philadelphia, allows students to attend workshops and gain hands-on experience with new educational products and applications.

Levin did not begin as a technology teacher. He was a sixth-grade social studies teacher when he first arrived at Prince Hall School. He began to use a single computer in his own course in 1982; soon, both he and his students were hooked. When he saw how the computer captured the interest and imagination of his students, he decided that he would make certain that computers would be available to all students.

By 1994 he was in charge of a computer lab that contained 44 computers, from Apple IIs to MAC LC 575s with built-in CD-ROMs, five printers, a laserdisc player, and a large-screen TV. He also provided Apple IIs and software to families to take home on loan. He had assembled all of this equipment and software through grants, fundraising, and money provided by community organizations and individuals.

Levin is a man on fire. He has seen how the use of computers has transformed the attitudes of the children who attend the school and their parents, and he will not rest until he has an adequate number of computers in every classroom at Prince Hall School. Watching how computers have improved student interest in learning and positively affected how teachers teach has transformed Levin and all who work with him. He is helping transform American schools.

There are many people like Mel Levin in American schools, people with enormous commitment who are ready to take charge if given the opportunity, who have more ideas for improving schooling than one can imagine, and who lack only the tools, the training, and the support required to change the way they do their jobs.

If these are the revolutionaries, who are their leaders? The answer is the leadership circle is large and consists mainly of classroom teachers and administrators. Most do not operate on a national stage, but they have enormous influence within their regions and states.

There are some individuals who are greatly admired by technology users, known nationally, and from whom teachers take inspiration, but they can scarcely be called "leaders," if that term means teachers must be followers. Following is a sample of the kinds of people these revolutionary teachers admire.

Tom Snyder is known and respected not only for his work; he also serves as a fantasy for many teachers. A former teacher, Snyder started his own company, Tom Snyder Enterprises, that produces software for schools. He is also an inspirational speaker who is in touch with problems teachers confront.

Therese Mageau edits *Electronic Learning,* one of the journals followed closely by teachers who wish to learn what other teachers are doing with technology and what new products are available. Mageau helps teachers stay abreast of the revolution.

Saul Rockman may be described as the conscience of the revolution. An independent researcher living in California, Rockman is respected as an evaluator of experimental projects and initiatives. He is one of the least likely people in the world to use hyperbole in anything; he is trusted by teachers because he is sincerely interested in helping them use technology successfully in ways that make sense educationally.

Every revolution needs a James Mecklenburger. Mecklenburger presents the issue of technology to every group he meets. Some years ago, while working for the National School Boards Association, he persuaded NSBA to create the Institute for the Transfer of Technology in Education (ITTE). The institute created a network of technology-innovative schools, launched a newsletter, organized one meeting a year at the Infomart in Dallas, and scheduled other meetings throughout the year on various technology topics that were held at schools that were using that technology. Although he is no longer at NSBA, Mecklenburger has established his own consulting organization.

Two practitioners are immensely popular not only because they have fresh ideas and are charismatic personally, but because they continue to see the world from the classroom teacher's point of view. They are Robert Pearlman, director of research for the Boston Teachers Union, and Alan November, technology coordinator for the Glenbrook, Illinois, schools.

My choice in government is Linda Roberts, a former classroom teacher who produced several important studies on technology use in schools on behalf of the Office of Technology Assessment. In 1993 she moved to join the U.S. Department of Education as Secretary Richard Riley's Special Advisor on Education and Technology. Technology teachers view her as their "friend in high government office." It is obvious from listening to her that she sees herself as the champion of those teachers who are trying to use technology wisely.

These are not the only people revolutionary teachers admire, but they are good examples. They share some common characteristics: 1) They are not running the revolution; they serve as sources of advice and inspiration and little more. They are seen as colleagues by the teachers; 2) They are not people widely known outside of the field of technology in education; and 3) None is a university professor. These leaders' characteristics and how teachers relate to them make this school reform different. It is being run from the inside rather than the outside.

Where is the Revolution Taking Place?

The revolution is occurring most often in individual classrooms, less frequently in entire schools, and seldom in entire school districts. We shall look at examples of each location.

Classrooms

Bill Burrall is a computer literacy and French instructor at Moundsville Junior High School in West Virginia.[2] His students participate in the AT&T Learning Network, a commercial telecommunications network that links students in learning circles in classrooms throughout the world. One feature of learning circles is establishing pen pals, leading students to communicate with one another by electronic mail rather than by postal services.

Because Moundsville Junior High School is within walking distance of the West Virginia penitentiary, some of the students became curious about the prison and about the lives of people living there. This led Burrall to contact prison authorities who produced prison pen pals for Burrall's students. Soon his students were exchanging candid notes with the prisoners, and their exchanges were further communicated to others on the Learning Network. Not only Burrall's students but others were exposed to the lives of people who had committed crimes and who had poignant advice to offer students so that they might avoid the problems that they had confronted. Burrall has found a way to give his students realistic exposure to a side of life he hopes they will never encounter firsthand.

Antoinette Kranning is a fifth- and sixth-grade teacher in Leopold, Indiana, a small, community on the banks of the Ohio River. Kranning's students design many of their own instructional products, drawing upon Hypercard and other software. In 1993 Kranning learned that children in the Upper Peninsula of Michigan were engaged in similar activities. She asked whether Indiana University's Center for Excellence in Education would make its teleconference facility available to her students, enabling them to talk to the students in Marquette, Michigan. One winter day in 1993, Kranning arrived by school bus with her students and principal. After no more than five minutes of instruction on how to use the keyboard that controls the cameras, the students were allowed to conduct their own professional meeting. The students exhibited their products and offered critiques of each other's work, seeking advice from one another. They carried on a professional meeting that was equivalent to what adults might have done. These Leopold students, because they had a revolutionary teacher, equipment, and support of a proud principal, were able to accomplish tasks far beyond those typically expected of that grade level.

Sherry Clark from Peters Township Middle School in McMurray, Pennsylvania, decided to take advantage of the TV monitors that had been placed in her school.[3] Her students established *The Peters Township Middle School*. The news show is broadcast within the school and to the community through the local cable company. Students write the content, and produce and anchor the news broadcasts, which consists of local/national news, sports, editorials, weather, school events, and book reviews. Student reporters have even covered an open-heart surgery of an earthworm in biology class. These students are engaged in activities that strengthen their skills in writing and speaking. The broadcasts are also good for school/community relations.

These are samples of hundreds of activities taking place in classrooms all over the country. They are reported regularly in such journals as *Electronic Learning, Electronic School,* and *T.H.E. Journal* read by teachers who use technology. None of the activities described above is designed for the purpose of teaching students about computers and other technology; students use the equipment to serve larger purposes and to achieve their own goals. All of these teachers are promoting the kind of active learning envisioned by the school reform movement.

Schools

The *Saturn School of Tomorrow*, led by Tom King and located in the center of St. Paul, Minnesota, is a magnet school that has taken advantage of technology to provide a very different kind of schooling experience.[4] The name itself, inspired by the Saturn automobile that was intended to launch an entirely new way of producing automobiles in America, is a signal that this school is different.

The school opened in the fall of 1989, serving 162 fourth-, fifth-, and sixth-grade students from all over St. Paul; it represents the ethnic mix of the city as a whole and includes students with special education needs. By 1995 the school had expanded to serve more than 300 students ranging across grades one through eight.

The original mission of the school was stated: "To bring together the best of what's known about effective learning research and powerful learning technologies into a restructured, transformed, personalized school setting that employs a Personal Growth Plan for each student, a curriculum for today and tomorrow, and the assumption of learning success for each child."

The heart of the Saturn concept is to enable students to design and complete their own Personal Growth Plans, which set out their own learning goals. These plans are negotiated with teachers and the students' parents. Throughout the year the students review their plans with their parents and teachers. Students can even ask for new courses to be added to the curriculum in order to meet their plans and interests. Students also pursue individual projects, drawing upon the resources of the St. Paul community.

Saturn is a technology-rich school. The backbone of the school is a network of 90 Macintosh machines that are available throughout the building to students and staff. Every learning space is equipped with a networked Mac, a videodisc player, a monitor for the school's communication network, and a telephone linked to the school's voice mail system. In addition, the school has employed Integrated Learning Systems for reading, math, and other topics. The school also uses LEGO/logo systems for computer programming and robotics, videodisc systems for access to high quality video libraries and sources, and the Discourse System for group-based instruction.

Students create portfolios to exhibit their work, drawing upon the technology to exhibit what they have accomplished. On the day I visited the Saturn School, students were in the last days of production of a video about the school itself. This was scheduled to be shown locally by one of St. Paul's TV stations.

The *ACT Academy* is a nontraditional, multiaged (5-18), multiability school serving 250 students in McKinney, Texas, a community approximately 20 miles north of Dallas.[5] The ACT (Academic Competitiveness through Technology) Academy resulted from a two-year, $5.5 million grant from the U.S. Secretary of Education's Fund for Innovation in Education. The purpose of the grant was to "create a school of the future" and then use the school as a laboratory for providing further training for teachers and administrators in the McKinney Independent School District. The grant was awarded in the fall of 1992. The director, Linda Farley, was recruited from the Minnesota Educational Computer Corporation (MECC) in Minneapolis. She and the staff began to plan the school in January 1993, and it opened to students for the first time in the fall of 1993.

The ACT Academy is located in a red-brick, white-trimmed building within a modest residential neighborhood. The original part of the building was constructed in 1910; other rooms were added in 1935. The major remodeling that took place in 1993 not only refurbished the building but also added the cables, outlets, and power that would enable it to function as a showcase for applications of technology in education. The design of the school fits the school's philosophy: both open and closed space, allowing for greater flexibility. The design also permits the portability of computers and other technologies; for example, the hallways and outer courtyard have been wired for access to the network.

The academy's curriculum and instruction are based upon constructivist theories of learning, embodied in six tenets:

- Students are active learners who construct knowledge based on prior experiences, values, and beliefs.

- Learning must move beyond factual recall to deep conceptual understanding of topics.

- Students bring to the learning process their own notions, myths, and ideas of particular concepts. These must be identified and valued with opportunities provided for students to evaluate, modify, and strengthen [them] based on new experiences.

- Learning extends beyond the four walls of the classroom through the use of technology, mentorships, internships, and local and national resources.

- Assessments and evaluations are embedded in the learning process and are an integral component of all activities and projects. Student growth and learning are measured against a standard, not against other students.

- Curriculum development is a dynamic and on-going process based on major concepts and consisting of an elaboration of students' interests and needs.

These six, life-long learning standards were developed with input from the community. The academy also uses the national subject area standards being developed by various academic disciplines. The instructional program is delivered through both single discipline and interdisciplinary content applications.

The academy works deliberately to employ technology to meet its instructional goals, and it has a wide range of technology at its disposal. For example:

- An ethernet and local talk network have been installed in the school with data drops in every room and common space, including the courtyard. This allows students and teachers (called facilitators at the academy) to gain access to printers, servers, e-mail, and net modems from anywhere in the building. Dial-in services allow students to retrieve ACT resources from outside of the school.

- All major learning areas have Macintosh and IBM computers that are compact-disc capable. Laserdisc players, VCRs, laser printers, and TV monitors are available in the learning areas.

- Facilitators have their own Macintosh Powerbook or IBM ThinkPad with fax modem.

- Students in the 7-11 age level have portable computers at a ratio of two students for each computer that may be checked out for home or field use. Students in the 12-18 age level have computers at one student per one computer ratio.

- Camcorders, still-video cameras, scanners, LCD projectors, overhead projectors, boom boxes, tape recorders, 35mm cameras, electronic copy boards, video visualizers, cable TV access, and satellite programming are also available for student and facilitator use.

- In addition to productivity software such as word processing, databases, and spreadsheets, ACT students have access to a wide variety of content software through the school's network.

The academy began its second year of operations in the fall of 1994. While it was still improving its own procedures, it had begun to offer professional training programs for teachers and administrators from other schools in the McKinney Independent School District. Those who want to study an effort to merge technology with school reform notions and constructivist learning theories should monitor the development of the ACT Academy.

Christopher Columbus School[6] is an intermediate school serving seventh- and eight-grade students in Union City, New Jersey. Union City is located in northern New Jersey's Hudson County, near the western entrance to the Lincoln Tunnel and a ten-minute drive from New York City. Union City, the most densely populated city in the United States (42,000 residents per square mile), is second only to Miami in its concentration of Latino residents (75.6 percent). The majority of residents are of low and moderate income. Nearly 80 percent of the district's students receive free or reduced price lunches, a figure that is three times greater than the national average.

In 1989 the New Jersey State Education Department considered taking over the Union City schools because of their poor performance. Out of 52 criteria that the state considered in its evaluation, the district schools were failing in 40. Student attendance, dropout and transfer rates, as well as scores on standardized tests were below state averages. Eventually, the state gave the Union City school district five years to improve itself.

In the years that followed, the school district revamped its curriculum and redesigned its approach to instruction; it changed the school board and brought in new administrators; it opened kindergartens in the elementary grades and moved seventh and eighth graders from two overcrowded elementary schools into a new middle school, the Christopher Columbus School.

Christopher Columbus Middle School opened in the fall of 1993 in a 100-year-old building that had once housed St. Michael's Grammar School. At first glance, this three-story, white stucco building appears to be very traditional, not much different from hundreds of other urban schools built about the same time. But visitors know this school is different from the moment they enter its front door. Not only is the building sparkling clean and freshly painted, but there is an aura of professionalism that is felt from the principal's office, through the hallways, and classrooms, to the library. What makes this school different? Strong leadership, a restructured curriculum, an energized staff, commitment to teacher professional development (40 professional development days in 1993/94), and exceptional access to technology, made possible largely by Bell Atlantic, are some of the major factors.

Bell Atlantic made a two-year commitment, beginning in the fall of 1993, to help Columbus become a model technology school. Bell wired the three-story building, provided personal computers for each classroom, supplied a remote server that offers a virtual CD-ROM library, arranged for electronic connections to Department of Defense schools overseas, supplied professional training workshops, and made other technology and software available to the school. In addition, it provided a personal computer, a telephone line, and modem to all seventh graders and their teachers, so that they could communicate with each other while working at home. The school board responded by adding Macintoshes to classrooms and by equipping a Macintosh lab.

This is not a school where one might expect to find a model program. The district is poor. For 95 percent of the students English is a second language and the school district once had the reputation of being one of New Jersey's worst. The combination of good leadership, a vision of the kind of school they wanted to become, support for staff development, and Atlantic Bell's philanthropy have made this a remarkable school. After only one year the results were positive. The eighth grade students in the Columbus School were the only students in the district in 1994 to meet New Jersey's Early Warning Test (EWT); in the practice EWT administered to seventh graders, Columbus students had the highest overall scores in the district. The Columbus School holds the district's best attendance record for both students and faculty and it had the fewest number of students transfer out and the highest number to transfer into the school. The Columbus School is demonstrating that it is possible to show remarkable gains even when the demographic variables are not in one's favor.

What do these three schools have in common? All began as special, model, or demonstration schools intended to carry out many of the principles of school restructuring and constructivist learning. All are rich in technology and use the technology to meet school reform initiatives. All were very expensive and could not exist without special grants. When schools are created as model schools, there is a tendency to provide every imaginable piece of technology available in order to ensure a full demonstration. Furthermore, without knowing in advance how much technology is enough, the instinct is to provide more than enough. These schools exhibit what can be accomplished if availability of technology is not an issue. They do not always provide a model for schools who must enter the Information Age without special grants or subsidies.

School Districts

Given the cost of equipping a single school with adequate equipment, it should be obvious why there are few school districts that have made district-wide commitments to a similar level of technology infusion for all of their schools. Nearly any school can provide for the needs of a single teacher; with outside grants and special set-aside funds, it is usually possible to take care of an entire school, but to meet the needs of an entire school district requires true commitment and long-range planning. Fortunately, there are some examples of school districts where this is occurring.

In 1990 the *Forest Hills Public Schools* in Grand Rapids, Michigan, formed an Advisory Committee on Technology, made up of 50 educators, parents, and business leaders.[7] The group recommended seven principles:

1. Develop student skills in problem solving, critical thinking, and analysis and management of information;

2. Enable students to become comfortable with technology and understand that the technologies are merely tools to assist them in performing their work;

3. Focus students' attention on using technologies as tools to extend knowledge and to individualize learning;

4. Develop an active participatory learning process;

5. Integrate all of the preceding principles into all grades and all disciplines;

6. Provide a climate receptive to change; and

7. Assist teachers in changing their roles from presenter of information to that of learning facilitator or coach.

With these principles in mind, the school system floated a special bond issue in 1990 in order to buy equipment and create technology infrastructure for its various buildings.

What is striking about the Forest Hills plan is how elements for elementary grades, middle grades, and high schools all fit together so that the skills in the use of technology build upon one another across grade levels and are exploited in each subject field. For example, keyboarding, word processing, and desktop publishing are first introduced in the upper-elementary grades. By the time students reach high school, all of the English teachers expect students to use these tools in preparing compositions and research papers. Students are first introduced to accessing databases in the middle schools. By the time they are in high school they are expected to use databases as part of their routine class work. For example, ninth-grade science classes use online weather data and social studies classes employ domestic and foreign news databases. Similar streams of training are employed to teach students the use of spreadsheets, graphics, communications, programming, and problem solving tools. All are introduced for the first time in elementary or middle schools and then carried forward and amplified in the secondary grades.

An especially interesting feature is a required course in mass communication for all high school students. This course combines skills and knowledge in writing and media production. Knowledge gained from the course has practical benefit in other classes, as students are expected to make reports that employ production techniques learned in mass communication. For example, one assignment for a group of students in the U.S. Government class was to prepare a 45-minute presentation as if they were staff members to Third District Congressman Vern Ehlers. Their job was to inform Congressman Ehlers on issues confronting his constituents, using presentation technology including computer images, videotape, audiotape, transparencies, television, and other devices. In addition, they were to develop written materials for all students in the class as well as any guests that were invited to the presentation. In order to create the report, students interviewed people in the community and employed technology in order to retain the substances of the interviews.

The mass communications class also provides the training for students who produce a ten-minute *Communication Break* each morning. This is a live video broadcast that goes to all classrooms. The main purpose of the program is to convey important announcements and messages to all of the students and staff. Students who produce the program are encouraged to use their own creativity.

What is striking about the Forest Hills plan is that the school district leaders have a vision of what their schools should be and the skills and knowledge their students must possess by the time they leave high school. They have linked their schools together in common cause behind that vision, have modified their curriculum accordingly, and are using the technology to fulfill that vision. Technology is crucial to their plan because they envision a world in which the ability to use technologies is critical. And they use the technology throughout the curriculum, rather than in set-aside courses on computer literacy, because it makes the use of the technology more authentic to the world outside of the school.

The *Central Kitsap School District,*[8] located in Silverdale, Washington, across Puget Sound from Seattle, is an example of a school district that began planning for technology in the early 1980s. While its plans have changed over time, as conditions changed and the staff gained experience, the fundamentals have remained constant. The Central Kitsap experience demonstrates the importance of having a well-conceived plan, of gaining the support of the community, teachers, and administrators, and of persisting from year to year in fulfilling the plan.

The school district's planning began in 1985 when the school board was faced with the prospect of designing two new elementary schools to accommodate rising enrollments. Rather than erect buildings similar to others in the district, the school board appointed a committee of parents, teachers, and others, gave each of them a copy of John Naisbitt's book, *Megatrends,* and asked them two questions: How should a school be designed to meet the needs of students in 2020, and how can technology achieve these ends? The result was a plan called Strategy 2020, a planning effort by educators and others in the community that established the principles for the two new schools. Among the initial principles agreed to were:

*"Join me in welcoming our new staff members, Mr. Simpson, art.
Ms. Dawes, science. Mr. Siblert, computer repairman."*

- Administrative and educational decisions should be made at the lowest level, preferably by teachers and students;

- Teachers should become managers of instruction, not just presenters of information;

- "My classroom is my castle" must be discarded as a guiding principle. Teachers should function as teams of professionals, sharing ideas and communicating frequently;

- Students should become more actively involved in their own learning, both individually and in groups; and

- Technology should be employed to "manage learning as well as diagnose, present, and evaluate" it.

Cougar Valley was the first technology-infused school in the district. The building opened in 1989 with a networked computer at each adult's workstation, a telephone in each classroom, five-to-six networked computers in each classroom, a 25-station computer lab, and VCRs, camcorders, a light table, and laser-disc player in the library. Technology was mostly defined as computers; the focus was on networking.

The result was both a delight and a disappointment. On the one hand, students were enthusiastic about the technology and were able to undertake tasks not possible previously. On the other hand, the file servers did not communicate easily with each other; software was not compatible with the system; there were too few telephone lines; and when the system failed to work properly, teachers and students became discouraged and ignored the technology available to them. At first, the district provided very little technical support to Cougar Valley; it had no one on its staff who even understood the network it had installed.

The next school, Silver Ridge Elementary School, opened in 1990. The district tried to apply lessons from Cougar Valley's experience. The staff was hired 15 months before the school opened, allowing them time to prepare for how they would teach in new ways appropriate to a modern new facility. The district hired technical support staff to work with the faculty in selecting hardware and software. The definition of technology was broadened to include video.

Silver Ridge opened with a networked computer at each adult's work station, a telephone in each classroom, and four networked centers in pod areas with 25-30 student computers in each center. Each classroom had a "teaching wall" that included a 25" monitor, a VCR, and a light table. Computers, VCRs, camcorders, laser-disc players, Xap-shot cameras, scanners, and CD-ROM players were placed in the library and each instructional pod. The school had a school-wide video distribution system as well as video-editing capabilities.

The results were better. Technical support was provided to train both teachers and students; certain students were assigned to "boot up" the computers each day and to make certain all other equipment was functioning. Placing the computers and multimedia devices in a common area serving several teachers worked well. It gave students ample access, while providing supervision.

In 1993 the district opened a third school, Emerald Heights. This school was able to take advantage of both the Cougar Valley and the Silver Lake experience. The staff was hired before the building opened in order to plan its use. Software selection was part of the curriculum and instructional planning process. While the range and deployment of technology is similar to that of Silver Lake, the district was able to purchase more powerful computers for its students.

While the emphasis in this description has been on new schools, the district has also brought older schools online and provided training to those faculty. According to Superintendent Janet Barry, by 1996 Central Kitsap will have spent $18 million on technology infrastructure. They will have placed between 120 and 250 networked student computers into every school and will have provided one computer per employee. They have placed video broadcast systems in five schools, and provided staff to support technology and to offer training to teachers. Clearly, Central Kitsap has made a long-term commitment to the use of technology to transform instruction.

While Forest Hills and Central Kitsap, described above, reached somewhat different conclusions about what needed to be done, they both began by developing plans that would guide their efforts over many years. The planning process involved not only teachers and other school staff but also leaders in the community beyond the school. Broad community support for a long-range plan is needed to avoid quick changes in direction following a new school board election or a change in superintendents. Finally, the plan gives structure to the long-term investment required in order to provide the required technology.

Who Supports the Revolution?

We have examined where the revolution is occurring—in classrooms, in individual schools, and across entire school districts. But revolutions require supporters, those who lend legitimacy as well as political and financial support to the revolution. Who supports the technology revolution in schools? Nearly everyone with influence believes in the potential of technology to influence education. The list includes government, business, and professional associations. Let's look at each in order to observe the contributions they are making.

Government

During the administrations of Presidents Ronald Reagan and George Bush, there was little effort to promote technology in schools. The U.S. Department of Education was more or less neutral on the issue, preferring other solutions, mainly vouchers and school choice, as the keys to school reform. Whether this was a result of a negative judgment about the role technology might play, or merely a reluctance to adopt policies that would require additional public funding, is difficult to say. Nevertheless, from time to time the federal government did play a role. For example, the *Star Schools Program* was launched as a Congressional initiative in the 1980s; it sparked many distance learning initiatives in schools. The National Science Foundation funded several research and development projects that tested new approaches to technology in schools, especially the use of electronic networks. And one of the last acts of the Bush administration was to fund the ACT Academy in the McKinney School District in Texas.

Those interested in the role of technology in education expected more attention from the Clinton administration. By 1994 there had been little money invested in education technology, but advocates seemed confident more would be done in the future. Secretary of Education Richard Riley's appointment of Linda Roberts as his special advisor for technology was important symbolically; it offered hope that technology issues would be given a priority in the Department of Education's plans. P.L. 103-227 *Goals 2000: Educate America Act* authorized Richard Riley to undertake a number of steps, including the development of a National Long-Range Technology Plan, aimed at strengthening the role of technology in school reform. Perhaps of equal importance have been discussions and proposed legislation around the notion of a National Information Infrastructure, the so-called electronic superhighway, as well as proposals to alter regulation of the telephone industry. What is less clear is how schools will gain access to high-speed national communication networks at affordable prices. Interest in using widely dispersed databases, by means of both commercial and Internet services, is growing rapidly among schools. Schools want to employ the services that will be provided by such networks; however, it may be that only the wealthiest school districts will be able to afford them.

Some governors have demonstrated a strong commitment to educational technology. The National Governors Association is on record as favoring increased use of technology in schools, and individual governors compete among themselves over who has the newest or best technology program. In 1983 Indiana established the Consortium for Computer and High Technology Education, which guided the introduction of computers into Indiana schools. Under a new administration, headed by Governor Evan Bayh, the consortium expired, and leadership was handed off to the Corporation for Educational Technology. Similar efforts could be cited for every state. In 1994 efforts underway in Kentucky, linking technology to the restructuring of the entire educational system, appeared to be the most extensive and promising.

Supporting the use of technology in schools is considered to be a good and politically safe thing to do in every state. Fully funding technology is another matter, as each state worries about balancing expenditures against income.

Business and Industry

American business and industry are strong supporters of the technology revolution in schools. Why? First, this is one school reform issue business leaders fully understand and whose benefits can be measured. Many other ideas disappear in the fog of education jargon; however, most business leaders have experience in employing modern technology to increase efficiency, improve customer relations, and profits. While a CEO of a Fortune 500 company will assume that the problems are different in schools, he nevertheless believes that if technology can make a difference in every other aspect of life, it can make a difference in schools as well. And he is right!

"I made it through mainstreaming, busing, teacher burnout, and state and local cut-backs. Just when things looked brighter, along comes 'The Software Search.'"

Not only have many business leaders become active in their own communities to promote the use of technology, but their national organizations have promoted technology applications in education as well. Most notable have been the Business Roundtable, the National Alliance for Business, and the Council for Aid to Education.

A second reason for business interest is that some business sectors stand to gain substantially if schools adopt technology and change the way they work. In the 1980s, IBM, Apple, Tandy, Pioneer, Panasonic and other firms selling computers and computer-based products made substantial contributions in money and equipment to encourage the use of technology. Telecommunication firms such as AT&T, GTE, MCI, and the "regional Bells" have become more visible in the 1990s because they believe that distance-learning applications as well as access to databases will be carried to schools and homes by means of their cables and wires. They will profit as schools begin to use technology more.

We should welcome participation by business firms in the technology revolution in schools, whatever their motives might be. Teachers have learned to look at gifts carefully in order to make certain they have not been saddled with an obligation greater than the value of the gift; they are eager to have the funds and equipment as well as the political support that typically accompanies the gift.

Professional Organizations

Professional organizations must respond to the interests of their constituents. They play an important role in helping members within the profession to decide on which side of an issue it is best to be found.

It is important to distinguish among the traditional, mainline educational organizations and those that have been recently established to represent the interest of the teacher technologists. I shall touch on both kinds of organizations briefly.

The American Federation of Teachers and the National Education Association are the two major unions representing teachers. It is often asserted, correctly or not, that school reform has been thwarted by the uncompromising attitudes of the unions and their desire to protect member interests. With regard to the use of technology in schools, both AFT and NEA are strong supporters of technology for education. Albert Shanker, AFT president, often speaks in support of technology in education. Robert Pearlman, of the Boston Teachers Union, is a leader in the effort nationally. The NEA has created the National Foundation for the Improvement of Education, headed by Gary Watts. One of its projects is *Learning Tomorrow*, which supports and stimulates the use of technology in restructured schools.

Both unions have concerns: They don't want technology to be used to replace teachers; they want to ensure that there is equity in the allocation of equipment and that teachers are given adequate training and support. But the unions are not opposed to the use of technology in schools; indeed, they are avid supporters.

What about administrators? The Council of Chief State School Officers has a major technology initiative underway and has recruited Frank Withrow, technology specialist from the Department of Education, to lead its efforts. The National School Boards Association has been a leader in encouraging technology use in schools for more than a decade. NSBA hosts the Institute for the Transfer of Technology in Education, sponsors conferences, and publishes materials designed to assist its members in employing technology wisely. The American Association for School Administrators (representing superintendents), the National Association of Secondary School Principals, and the National Association for Elementary and Middle School Principals are all solidly behind the use of technology as part of the school reform strategy.

Important journals like *Educational Leadership*, published by the Association for Supervision and Curriculum Development (ASCD), and the *Phi Delta Kappan* are read by teachers, administrators and educational policy makers all over the nation. While the editors are obligated to treat many issues in education, they frequently carry articles relating to the theme of technology in education, thereby lending credibility and support to the revolution.

Professional associations that attract teachers from subject matter disciplines—e.g., National Council for the Social Studies, National Council for Teachers of Mathematics, National Science Teachers Association—provide avenues through their publications and conferences for teachers to become familiar with the use of technology in their disciplines. At annual meetings these associations sometimes set aside rooms where teachers can gain firsthand experience in using one or more of the hardware or software tools appropriate to their discipline.

In addition to the older, more established professional associations, new ones have been founded in recent years. In Indiana, two organizations serve teachers and supervisors with a special interest in technology. Hoosiers Educational Computing Consortium (HECC) serves computer coordinators especially, and Indiana Computer Educators (ICE) attracts a broad membership of teachers who are using computers and other technology in their teaching. There are counterpart organizations in most other states.

At the national level the most prominent organization is the International Society for Technology in Education based in Eugene, Oregon. It has approximately 40,000 members and publishes two journals, *Learning and Leading with Technology* and the *Journal of Research on Computing in Education,* as well as a newsletter, special-interest periodicals, and books and courseware designed for classrooms. It is the administrative sponsor of the well-managed and well-financed National Education Computing Conference (NECC), which draws nearly 6,000 revolutionaries.

Teacher education has been slow to react to growth in the use of technology by teachers. Some teacher educators even appear to take a smug satisfaction in their ignorance of technology. The editor of one of the leading teacher education journals introduced a special theme issue on technology by saying, "I readily admit to being a technology-phobe. For example, although I thoroughly enjoy playing a variety of computer games, I have almost religiously avoided any sort of work on computers. . . . The presence of computers in every office and VCRs in every home has begun to sensitize even a Luddite such as me."

I don't quote the editor because his position is outrageous, but because it is typical. However, there is a growing group of teacher educators who are concerned about technology in education, who find that the American Association for Colleges of Teacher Education (AACTE) and the Association for Teacher Educators (ATE) do not meet their needs, and who have established a new organization called the Society for Technology and Teacher Education. It publishes the *Journal of Technology and Teacher Education* and the *Technology and Teacher Education Annual,* containing the papers presented at its annual conference.

All in all, the professional associations support the revolution in technology education. There is no organized opposition from that quarter.

Colleges and Universities

With some exceptions, colleges and universities have been unconnected to the school reform movement. Unlike the 1960s, when many universities were creating materials reflecting the academic disciplines or offering institutes for teachers, the influence of colleges and universities has been missing. One can cite exceptions, such as the Center for Educational Renewal, headed by John Goodlad at the University of Washington; the Coalition for Essential Schools and the Annenberg Institute for School Reform, headed by Ted Sizer and based at Brown University; James Comer's School Development Program at Yale University; Henry Levin's Coalition for Accelerated Schools at Stanford University; and Robert Slavin's Center for Research on Effective Schooling for Disadvantaged Students at Johns Hopkins University. All five of these are based at universities in part because that is where the director holds an academic appointment. It is difficult to judge the degree to which the project and the university have much impact on one another.

There have been no equivalent organizations for technology in schools. Until recently, one of the most prominent has been Bank Street College of Education, which has conducted research on technology in education for more than a decade and which once hosted the U.S. Department of Education Center on Educational Technology. MIT is known for its Media Lab as well as for Seymour Papert, inventor of Logo and the source of many ideas relating to the use of technology in education. His book *Mindstorms* has influenced many in the field. Vanderbilt University has built a group around the cognitive psychologist John Bransford. Northwestern University provides a home for The Institute for the Learning Sciences, headed by Roger Shank. The Center for Excellence in Education at Indiana University, while a latecomer to the field, has initiated programs and activities to contribute to the field.

While there are many professors across the nation who teach courses in computer literacy or consult with schools on one technology project or another, the influence of universities on the use of technology for instruction is marginal at best. Teachers in training see few professors model technology for instruction in the liberal arts courses they take for general education and for their disciplinary majors. Even professors of education rarely employ new technology in their courses. The colleges and universities as a whole may be judged neutral in their influence on the technology revolution in schools.

Research and Development Organizations

Several independent organizations are creating products and testing ideas that find their way into classrooms. The Laboratory for Teaching and Learning at the University of Pittsburgh has been a longtime leader; other U.S. Department of Education labs, such as the North Central Regional Education Laboratory, have made contributions. Technical Education Research Centers (TERC) is a research and development center based in Cambridge, Massachusetts; it focuses principally on improvements in science and mathematics and has joined with National Geographic to create Kidsnet, a project that links elementary grade children within the United States and abroad by electronic mail. The Education Development Center hosts the Center for Children and Technology. Xerox established the Institute for Research on Learning in Palo Alto. This center is testing various ideas about how to link technology to learning theory. Other groups could be cited. While there are a few organizations that have used grants and contracts to develop products and services that may advance the field, none has a following equivalent to Ted Sizer's Coalition for Essential Schools. They are essentially research and development organizations, not sites for school reform.

Foundations

Foundations are the source of seed capital for innovations in education. Most of the money to support technology innovations in education has come from government sources such as the National Science Foundation and the Department of Education, and from business-related foundations— e.g., IBM, Apple, and AT&T. Sometimes the funds are provided by the philanthropic arm of the corporation; in other cases they originate from a separate foundation such as the AT&T Foundation.

The large private foundations that typically support educational reform—namely, Ford, Lilly, Kellogg, MacArthur, Carnegie, Rockefeller, Pew, and Danforth—have invested little in the technology revolution. The Ford Foundation, once a major backer of instructional television, appears to have lost interest in or confidence in educational technology. Why is this true? Perhaps, it is because the large foundations tend to invest in university-based research and development rather than in schools directly, and universities have shown little interest in reform through technology. Perhaps foundations are fearful of the amount of money that would be required to make a difference. Foundations do receive proposals from school systems regarding technology; the typical proposals seek money for equipment primarily. The foundations know if they begin making equipment grants, the amount of money they could be asked to spend could be limitless—or at least beyond their capacity. Some foundation officers also assert that they receive few proposals that demonstrate how the technology might actually impact on the curriculum and instruction. Several foundations have shown a readiness to invest in the "human side" of technology, in teacher education and faculty broadly. Yet the private foundations are largely on the sidelines with regard to the use of technology to reform schooling.

What are the Chances for Success?

We have substantial literature on educational change: how it occurs, how it spreads, and—all too frequently—why it fails. Most of this literature is based upon innovations created outside of the schools and imposed on them. The typical question facing educational reformers is how to win teachers' support for the reformer's idea in order to build commitment among teachers equal to that of the innovator. Schools often adopt ideas when funds are attached to their adoption, and drop the innovation once the funds have expired. The reason for this apparent fickleness is that schools need money, and they cannot know if the idea is worthwhile until they try it. If the idea fails to win devoted followers among the teachers, the schools reject the innovation as soon as possible. From the school's point of view, this is a rational way to behave.

The potential success of the educational technology revolution cannot be judged in the same way as other educational innovations. First, the movement is driven by teachers rather than by outside experts. Second, teachers are not required to use the technology in a prescribed way; they use it as they choose or reject it if they wish. Third, their students are eager to use technology, and parents want their children to have access to technology in school. Fourth, once teachers have overcome their initial concern about feeling stupid while they learn a new tool, they find themselves using the technology in various instructional situations. They are pleased to have learned a new skill, and they gradually change the way they teach. Because of these factors, I cannot imagine that this reform will fail for the same reasons as previous reforms.

The progress of technology in school will surely proceed more slowly than its proponents would prefer. The reasons are mainly time and money. While Americans talk expansively about "break the mold" schools, they want a cheap reform. They hope that by reorganizing the administration of schools, leading to "site-based management," or by allowing parents to choose schools for their children, school reform will be successful. They are wrong. These cheap solutions will have little impact. In contrast, enormous amounts of money will have to be spent on rewiring and equipping schools, and additional money must be devoted to staff training. It is not yet clear that Americans want new kinds of schools badly enough to pay for them.

Lack of money will slow the revolution—making it seem more like evolution—but it won't kill it. If you believe that schools are a part of the American culture, that American culture is increasingly influenced by Information Age technology, and that teachers participate in the American culture as much as other Americans, you cannot believe that teachers will use the technology outside of school but not employ it on the job. Technology *will* be used extensively in schools. It is inevitable.

Chapter 6

ACHIEVING SCHOOL REFORM THROUGH TECHNOLOGY

When you go to the hardware store to buy a drill, you don't actually want a drill. Instead you want a hole. They don't sell holes at the hardware store, but they do sell drills, which are the technology to create holes. We must not lose sight that technology—for the most part—is a tool and it should be used in applications which address educational concerns or problems. We should, therefore, focus on the appropriate application of the technology, rather than the tool itself.
Geoffrey H. Fletcher[1]

I have no doubt that the use of technology in schools will continue to grow; I am not equally certain that increasing technology use will lead to better schools and higher student performance. It should not be our purpose to see how much technology we can pack into classrooms. Our primary goal should be to help schools become places where students learn more effectively, and our secondary goal—related to and probably necessary for the first—is to make schools more interesting and rewarding places to work so that talented adults will become and remain teachers.

After decades of efforts to reform schools, it has become obvious to many that piecemeal reforms make little impact. The main problem is that our schools, which were once the envy of other nations, no longer serve us as well as in the past. The changes required are deep and fundamental, including how we teach youngsters, what they are taught, and how we measure the results of instruction. Such changes are not easy, because the stakeholders are not fully agreed on the degree and direction of changes required.

Technology can be the catalyst for considering wholesale change in schooling. Nearly everyone understands that to use technology effectively requires planning, teacher training, and technical support. As part of the process of planning for technology implementation, educators can ask each other such questions as: How can we teach more effectively using technology? What changes shall we make in our courses to take advantage of technology? Can we assess student work better if we use technology? Making technology the focus of the dialogue can remove the threat to established interests while providing the occasion to reconsider all of the ways that schools do their work.

The principal advantage for adopting technology in schools is not that it can help schools do better and faster what they have always done; its primary value is that it can provide the spark for reenergizing teachers, for prompting educators to envision new ways to teach, and for creating the kinds of schools needed now.

What are the reform ideas that schools should embrace? We have touched upon them at various times, earlier in this book, but a brief review of key elements may be useful. They include:

- A recognition that all children can and do learn, that most children can perform at higher levels of achievement than they do today, that children vary greatly in their readiness to learn, in what they need and want to learn and in the ways they learn best, and that schools must increasingly customize instruction, enabling each child to learn to the best of his or her ability.

- A commitment to make schools more interesting and challenging institutions for learning, where students take greater responsibility for their own education, and where instruction is more interactive, more collaborative, and more closely tied to authentic life experience than is currently the rule.

- A belief that schools must become more accountable to the public for their work and that with accountability comes the necessity to allow individual schools and school districts greater flexibility in how instruction will be provided.

- Acceptance that student and teacher assessments should become performance based and not rest solely upon degree attainment, experience, or time spent in courses.

While additional ideas could be added, these elements are widely accepted as the core of the current reform movement. Technology can—and already does in some schools—contribute to the success of each of these core elements. The precise ways that educators employ technology to reform schools vary widely. Conditions vary, and each school must take its own initiative. Nevertheless, technology can help supply the spark for reform in schools throughout the United States.

In the remainder of this chapter, I will propose four possible scenarios for how technology will influence schools during the next decade. I shall then draw on the research literature relating to school change to derive seven lessons that will help us to accomplish the changes we want. I shall conclude the chapter with advice to key stakeholders whose action is required if technology and school reform are to result in better schools.

Four Possible Scenarios for the Future of Schools

Thus far, I have commented in detail on what is happening or what should happen with regard to school reform. But what is likely to happen? Will technology actually transform schools? No one knows for certain, but the following four brief scenarios provide credible predictions. Which future we get depends mainly upon us.

Scenario No. 1: School is Out

I have named this scenario after the title of a book written by Lewis Perelman, published in 1992.[2] Perelman is a technology specialist who is frustrated because schools have been slow to take advantage of the opportunities provided by instructional technology. According to Perelman, "Computer-based instruction produces at least 30 percent more learning in 40 percent less time at 30 percent less cost, compared with traditional classroom teaching." In his view, schools are highly bureaucratized structures, interested primarily in saving jobs of educators and in soaking taxpayers, while denying students the learning they deserve.

Perelman believes schools are obsolete. While the public has not yet awakened to this fact, when they do, they will abandon the public schools. He compares schools to American railroads; they did not awaken quickly enough to what was happening to their business and are now a marginal part of America's passenger transportation system.

While writing this book, I came repeatedly upon a metaphor of a frog. I can no longer recall where I read it first—and I have made no independent effort to judge whether frogs actually behave as described, but this is the story. If one puts a frog into a pot of boiling water, presumably, it will sense the danger immediately and leap out. If a frog is placed in pleasantly warm water, and then someone gradually turns up the heat, the frog does not become aware of its danger until it is too late, causing it to be cooked alive.

Although Perelman believes that schools are like the frog slowly being boiled alive, I see it differently. While it is true that most schools are not yet using technology in ways that would advantage students and support school reform, it is not because they are being lulled to sleep. Nearly everyone is yelling "jump" at the schools. Most schools would jump if they could, and if the public could agree on where they should land.

Perelman uses the term hyperlearning to stand for all of the existing technology that enables students to learn on their own. In Perelman's view, such technology will soon prove so attractive to students and parents that they will withdraw students from public schools and allow them to work at home or enroll in alternative institutions. While he is scant on details regarding what the new institutions might be, how they would be organized, and so on, he believes that their advantages will become obvious to students and parents.

Perelman believes that the opportunities for students to learn are better than at any time in history, so long as they avoid public school. His prediction for schools is grim because he believes they will not take advantage of instructional technology until it is too late.

Scenario No. 2: The Tortoise Wins the Race

We know the fable about the rabbit and the tortoise. The rabbit is faster, looks better running, but is easily distracted. The tortoise stays the course, trudges along, and eventually wins. Reformers are like rabbits; they dazzle us with their ideas; but they are easily bored; they soon move on to new projects when their ideas are not rapidly adopted. Schools are like tortoises. They may change slowly, but they make progress. Outsiders may criticize them, or even force them to change in a particular direction, but left again on their own, the turtles proceed on their own path at a comfortable pace. In ten years, new reform rabbits will appear proclaiming new solutions for schools, but they will also quickly tire.

In this scenario, schools will add technology as they can afford it, but the funds provided will be too small to make a major difference in how schools do their work. The technology will be used variously, conforming largely to individual teacher's interests and ability—as is the case today. In short, five to ten years from now, schools will be very similar to the schools we have today, except that there will be a greater use of technology.

Scenario No. 3: The revolution has arrived!

It is possible that the American public will decide that American schools are their most precious public asset and that they have been neglected far too long. By public demand, both state and national legislators will appropriate funds that will modernize school buildings across the nation, equipping nearly all to the level only enjoyed by magnet or model technology schools today. Teachers and staff will be given all of the training required to take advantage of the technology, and the schools will have sufficient funds to employ the technical staff to maintain the technology. In addition, the incentives provided by new or remodeled facilities plus adequate technology will have led educators all over the nation to take proposals for change seriously.

The results will be spectacular. American schools will become the strongest institutions in American society. The Japanese and Germans will send delegations to the United States to study the "American education miracle." The brightest college students will become teachers; the schools will become learning centers for each community and be open from early in the morning to late at night, twelve months of the year, serving the learning needs of young and old alike. Students will work hard, enjoy school, and beat all comers in international academic competition. Ninety-eight percent of our youth will graduate from high school; 60 percent will begin, and 40 percent will complete four years of college. And those who do not attend college will find high-salaried, high-skilled jobs. As a result, business will be booming; the federal debt will be retired, and crime rate will have plummeted, leading to a plan to convert prisons and reformatories into retirement homes for those government officials who originally authorized their construction.

Does this sound like a dream? Some parts—like the retirement homes—may seem farfetched, but much of this scenario could be accomplished if there were sufficient will and persistence. For example, technology can make schools more interesting, challenging, and rewarding places for both students and teachers. Schools could become sites in each community where small firms could purchase employee training from schools during the hours regular classes are not in session. What is required is a vision of what public schools might become, coupled with a commitment and a plan to make it happen.

Scenario No. 4: The Market Prevails

It is 2005, and a majority of Americans have become so impatient with the tortoise-like pace of change in public schools that they have turned to their state legislatures for relief. The legislatures and courts have agreed that public money can be used for educational vouchers, allowing parents and students to spend public funds on whatever schooling they want; the courts have decided there can no longer be a public monopoly for public education. The choice movement has spread rapidly across the entire country; private firms have appeared that franchise schooling—K-8 at first, but later prekindergarten through high school.

Private schools have opened in modern new buildings or fully renovated former public school buildings. Some of the private schools fill their buildings with modern technology, employ some of the best, former public school teachers of each city at twice their former salaries, and round out the teaching force with unlicensed college graduates, teachers-in-training, and volunteers. The schools open early and close late to accommodate parents who drop off and pick up their children. The state pays three-fourths of the tuition; the parents the remaining fourth.

Although some public schools continue to exist, they serve mainly those who remain with them out of loyalty or because of extra curricular programs not provided in private schools, or because they have no other choice. Most legislators send their children to the new, private academies that have proven profitable. Legislators expect public schools to live within the same allocation of funds provided on a per-student basis to the private schools.

Scenario No. 4 resembles somewhat Scenario No. 1. Both imagine that the public schools are unable to meet the new demands placed upon them and lose the support of their most influential constituents. The scenarios offer a grim picture for the future of public education—a nightmare for public school officials and a dream for some business leaders and public officials.

While I think any of the four scenarios is possible and while I want the *revolution* to succeed, if forced to bet, I would put my money on Scenario No. 2, the *tortoise*. It is not that the revolution is beyond reach; I simply do not believe that the public is ready to invest the money required for reform to succeed. We have seen what can be done when schools undertake reform assisted by technology, but nearly all of the successful schools have been awarded special funds to support their unusual activity. There is little likelihood that similar investments will be made in all schools.

Scenario No. 1, *School is Out*, seems unrealistic to me, not because technology is incapable of satisfying Perelman's vision, but because most students want to go to school; they want to be with other children their age; and most parents do not want their children at home. They want them at school, especially if they believe the schools are safe and are truly interested in their children.

Scenario No. 4, private schools with public funds, is likely if the current school reform proves unsuccessful and if sentiment grows for a radical alternative. Perhaps, one-half or more American families could afford a private education for their children, if public funds were used to pay three-fourths of the cost, and most of the students who attended the private schools would likely prefer them to any of the public schools still available. It is difficult to imagine that the public schools could recover from a policy of public support to private education.

Seven Lessons From Research on School Change

During the past three decades, there has been considerable research on school change and why school reforms often fail and only occasionally succeed. Michael G. Fullan, dean of the Faculty of Education at the University of Toronto, and Matthew B. Miles, senior research associate with the Center for Policy Research, are two of the most respected scholars on this topic. In June 1992, they published an article, *Getting Reform Right: What Works and What Doesn't,*[3] in which they offered seven propositions for success. Presumably those who wish to reform schools by means of technology will be more successful if they adhere to these research findings.

I have quoted the title of each of their propositions and added my own commentary. Fullan and Miles are responsible for the propositions but cannot be blamed for my interpretations.

Lesson 1. Change is learning—loaded with uncertainty. Let us assume a teacher who has been teaching the same subject or grade level successfully for approximately a decade. Let us also assume that this teacher uses little instructional technology beyond an overhead projector, knows nothing about computers, and is unable to program her VCR. Let us also assume that the school board has adopted recommendations relating to school reform and has made a commitment to make computers widely available to both students and teachers. In return for this investment, the school board expects to see significant results in student learning and teaching effectiveness.

Imagine the steep learning curve that faces this teacher and the anxiety that is provoked by the new policy and resources. It is not likely that the teacher will be provided a paid leave to learn what she needs to know; rather, she will be expected to learn mainly on her own, except for possibly a few days of training on the equipment. Meanwhile, following a decade of teaching experience, our teacher has acquired knowledge, habits and teaching skills that appear to provide no advantage for her new assignment. She not only has to learn new skills, she may also have to discard attitudes and beliefs that she depended upon in the past. She will not be nearly so efficient in her work in the beginning; it will take her longer, for example, to prepare a test on the computer than when she composed it on a typewriter or wrote it out. Efficiency may come later, but only after the new skills are fully accomplished.

The change in role from teacher-presenter to teacher-facilitator is simple to state but difficult to accomplish. In the past, her job was primarily to organize the content of the material she wanted students to learn and then present the information. In the new role she has to be aware of a wide range of resources students can use; she has to be able to advise students on how to gain access to these resources; and she must be able to modify her instruction to fit individual interests and abilities within the class. The challenge she faces may seem greater to her than her first year of teaching.

In the ACOT experiment described in Chapter 4, the researchers found that teachers required three to five years before they became comfortable with the computers and their new roles. Other studies have reported similar results. Teachers involved in major reforms appear to pass through a number of stages, beginning with an ability to use the technology as directed, and progressing to a much later stage when the technology truly becomes a tool that they can use for whatever purpose they have.

The good news is that given enough time, teachers become thoroughly committed to the use of technology and to their new roles. It appears that the more difficult the learning task, the greater the teacher's commitment, once new skills and knowledge are under control. Having accomplished a major transformation, teachers take pride in what they have done, feel a greater sense of self-esteem, and are less likely to revert to prior practices.

Two important keys to encouraging teachers to undertake such tasks are 1) reducing the consequences of failure and 2) allowing adequate time to fully develop the new skill. If competent teachers are to be found incompetent because they cannot master new tasks quickly, there is little incentive to change. If administrators and colleagues are impatient with the time required to learn, teachers will quickly become discouraged and disillusioned.

If we want to have schools where students learn more, we must create conditions where teachers are encouraged to learn more as well.

Lesson 2. Change is a journey, not a blueprint. It is impossible to predict what will happen following the introduction of educational technology. While it is wise to have general plans in mind, flexibility must be the rule. Schooling, like life itself, can be chaotic and unpredictable: New opportunities arise; key players become ill, retire, or move on to new jobs and are replaced by people with new talent and skills.

The lesson is easily demonstrated by the way technology has been used in school in the past, even the reasons for employing technology have changed. Two decades ago it was important to provide students with computer literacy and to teach them how to program computers. Today these goals are seen as less important than having students use computers as tools for their own work.

Nearly everyone who advises schools on technology stresses the importance of their developing comprehensive plans indicating how the technology will be used, maintained, and replaced, how the curriculum will be modified, and so on. While such plans are important, it is equally important to revisit the plans periodically and revise them in view of unanticipated circumstances.

Lesson 3. Problems are our friends. Introducing change into schools causes problems within schools. Established interests are threatened as work becomes more complex and uncertain; this leads to greater stress on all who are involved. The major issue is not whether there are problems but how the problems are handled. Are they avoided? Are they dealt with superficially? Or does the school use problems to grow and become stronger?

The introduction of technology into schools leads to many problems teachers did not experience before. For example, whatever is claimed, the technology will not always work; the equipment will break or fail to function in the midst of a well-planned presentation. Unless the school is willing to treat such problems seriously and provide prompt technical support when it is needed, teachers will avoid depending upon certain tools after having one or more bad experiences using them. Second, most teachers require considerable training before they feel comfortable with new equipment; if the principal treats such insecurity as a teacher's problem rather than a school problem that he must help solve, teachers will often resolve their insecurity by not using the technology. Third, certain instructional problems that may seem trivial to some are annoying, nonetheless. For example, teachers may learn that certain tasks they once assigned students to perform in the library can be done in hours, using technology, rather than days of using more traditional library techniques; as a result, teachers may have to alter assignments and plan their courses differently. Each of these problems can frustrate teachers. The healthy school organization is one that treats problems as friends and tries to learn from them.

Lesson 4. Change is resource-hungry. Any kind of change requires additional resources for new staff, space, equipment, training, materials, and external consultants. The problem is exacerbated by the demands of new technology.

Let's start with the school buildings themselves. In 1995, the Government Accounting Office [GAO] released two reports pertaining to the condition of schools. The first, *School Facilities: Condition of America's Schools,*[4] estimated that $112 billion would be required simply to bring school facilities up to good overall condition. The second, *School Facilities: America's Schools Not Designed or Equipped for 21 Century,*[5] noted that more than half of America's schools lack the education technology infrastructure—electrical power, cabling, switches, servers, etc.—needed to support the technology requirements of schools.

Budgets must also be adjusted to pay for maintenance contracts, equipment replacements, and new services made possible by technology. Purchasing telecommunications equipment is merely the first expense that follows a decision to introduce distance learning; the telephone companies will charge service fees for each minute the programs operate. Furthermore, unless schools provide funds for high-quality courseware and software, the expensive computers they have purchased will sit idle most of the time.

Technical support should be a big item in school budgets. Schools should not expect that teachers will become technical experts. The school must either employ people or have outside technicians who can resolve technical problems quickly.

Funds are required for professional development—not just a two-day introductory workshop, but continuing training. Many teachers using computers today were forced to train themselves. This may have been sufficient for the vanguard, but it will not do for the troops. Patient, hand-holding training over several years will be required to help most faculty and staff reach a level of experience that will permit them to operate independently.

But the most important resource of all is time. According to Fullan and Miles, "Every analysis of the problems of change efforts that we have seen in the last decade of research and practice has concluded that time is the salient issue." More time is required of teachers: Time for planning, time for learning new skills, additional class preparation time; and more time is required for administrators to manage the change process. According to one study, the average school principal engaged in a school-wide reform effort spent 70 days a year on change management—32 percent of an administrator's year. We expect some overload when any reform is undertaken, but time requires energy, and unless provisions are made for how new time demands are to be met, the demands on time and energy will ultimately produce frustration and discouragement. Teachers and administrators will worry that everyday responsibilities are being slighted, and they will be unhappy that the reforms are less successful than expected. Time is even required to find the funds to support reform. Unless schools write proposals for external grants or engage in other fundraising activities, they are unlikely to obtain the funds needed to produce the reform results they want.

Lesson 5. Change requires the power to manage it. The first wave of school reform in the 1980s consisted mainly of new mandates, laws, and regulations. By 1989 it was apparent that these mandates were having little if any discernible effect. Mandates look good on paper; they attract the attention of the media; they give the appearance that reform is occurring when in fact nothing more than an edict was published.

The reform we want must occur in each classroom. Changing the roles of students and teachers and the relationship between the two roles cannot be ordered. They can only happen if teachers choose to make reform happen.

Site-based management is one of the key components of the current school reform movement. While this indicates a recognition that management authority needs to be tightly linked to where most of the activity occurs, we are far from developing good solutions to the decentralization of authority. On the one hand, reform is likely to fail unless the people who must carry it out have a voice in its development; on the other hand, school systems cannot tolerate hundreds of teachers making totally independent judgments about the curriculum for their students. Site-based management requires a level of consultation, coordination, and collaboration that is not expected or required in traditional schools.

Schools have been governed by top-down, hierarchically layered bureaucracies that allowed little room for decision making by teachers. Successful reform requires the development of new forms of decision making that provides a voice for the community, the elected board of education, administrators, teachers, students and parents. Collaboration and joint decision making are required not only to make these groups feel better because they were included; more importantly, they must be involved because the energy, time, and resources necessary to a successful reform require their commitment.

Finally, no reform, however well-planned, can anticipate all eventualities. Frontline workers must have sufficient understanding of mutually shared goals and must have gained sufficient trust of other players that they can confidently act independently when the occasion demands it.

Fortunately, sharing information is one arena in which technology has much to contribute. Technology is especially able to foster communication, maintain records, and keep track of things. It is easier to keep reform partners aware of what is taking place through technology.

Lesson 6. Change is systemic. Most attempts at innovation in schools have been shaped by a project mentality, in which a particular approach to instruction or a new set of curriculum materials is promoted and tested. The innovation is safe because only a few students or teachers are affected. Most such innovations do not survive their initial trial; if they are maintained, it is because a few individuals champion the cause and because the effects are scarcely felt elsewhere in the system. Whatever change occurs is relatively superficial.

What is being attempted today is a fundamental restructuring of schools, transforming the way they do their work, converting them from an industrial-age model to one more appropriate for the Information Age. The roles of the key players—students, teachers, administrators—are being redesigned to help each student reach his/her maximum potential. The goal is to customize schooling for individual learners rather than mass produce students who have essentially been taught the same thing in the same way in the same amount of time. This is not a superficial change; it is a deep cultural change.

To accomplish deep change it is necessary for all of the players to understand what is being attempted and to remain committed to a long-term strategy. For reform to succeed, it is not useful for new boards of education and/or new governors to sweep aside one set of reforms and replace it with another. Tactical changes are always necessary, but a vision of what the school of the future could and should become must be maintained.

Lesson 7. All large-scale change is implemented locally. Despite the best intentions of top-down reformers, change cannot be implemented from Washington, D.C., or from a state capitol. School reform will be interpreted at the local level, in each school district, school, and classroom. The reform of the Chicago Public Schools is not the same as the reform of schools in Bean Blossom, Indiana, or even in Indianapolis. This does not mean that federal and state government have no influence on reform priorities; indeed, their voice is often critical in starting and sustaining reform. But a formula that makes sense in a Washington office or a legislative committee room may seem like a message from another planet when it reaches the local community.

Public officials recently have encouraged the development of national goals and standards for each of the academic areas. Their stated intention is to provide benchmarks for schools regarding what students should know and teachers should teach. Opponents of this effort fear that this will lead to efforts at the state and national level to direct instruction in each classroom across the country. If this were to happen, the results would be predictable: anger and frustration.

The role of the reformer is to identify real (not imagined) problems, offer suggestions for how the problems might be resolved, encourage and inspire those who must solve the problems, and get out of the way. Reformers should expect their ideas to be changed to fit local circumstances. If ideas are not modified, only the language of the reform will be adopted.

Some Advice to Those Who Can Influence School Reform

I want to offer a few simple words of advice to those who are able to influence the success of the current school reform movement and who agree with me that strengthening the appropriate use of technology in schools is the key to successful reform. I wish to address school boards, school administrators, teachers, government, universities, and foundations.

School Boards Once a school board has agreed to undertake major school reform using technology, it is vital that everyone understands that this decision requires a long-term commitment if it is to be successful. To ensure the commitment is understood and met, the board must involve community opinion leaders and win their support. The public should be told what the additional costs are likely to be over the next several years; they also should be informed that they may not see a payoff for five years or more. Unless the board has broad community support, the plan can easily become unsettled following the election of new board members.

Before appropriating any money for technology, the school board should insist that the staff present the board with a strategic plan for how they propose to implement the technology. A plan that merely lists equipment and how it will be used is not adequate. A good plan will begin with a vision about what the schools should become over time; it should set forth the staff's goals for curriculum, instruction, and staffing. The plan should contain implementation procedures with benchmarks for each stage of development. While the board may wish to amend or alter the plan somewhat before it is finally approved, the plan ought to provide evidence that there is sufficient commitment and understanding by the staff to justify the expenditures.

In return for a well-developed plan, the board should be as generous as it can be in allowing time for the changes to occur and in providing funds for staff training, technical support, external consultants, software, and hardware. One rule of thumb is to set aside three percent of the total school budget, or 15 percent of the technology budget for staff training. If possible, the board should provide enough computers so that each teacher can have one at home as well as at school. Because teachers do much of their work at home outside of school hours, if they are to utilize technology fully, they need the equipment when and where they are going to work.

School Administrators Principals and superintendents provide overall leadership for school reform; they are the primary link between classroom teachers and the school board and the community. They are chiefly responsible for monitoring the results of the reform, providing information to the community, and explaining problems, successes, and failures.

Both superintendents and principals need to plan carefully how they will introduce technology into their schools and/or build upon prior acquisitions.

The pace of research and development is very rapid, making last year's purchases seem quickly out-of-date. It is therefore sometimes tempting to resist implementing technology until R&D stops or at least slows its pace. Unfortunately, this is not likely to happen in our lifetime; schools must begin to implement technology now, while recognizing that they will have to continue to add to and build upon their choices during the years ahead. Only in the most unusual circumstances is it possible to supply the technology requirements of all schools and all teachers at the same time.

Administrators should move as quickly as possible toward using technology for administrative tasks, such as using e-mail to communicate, televising school board meetings over local access cable channels, connecting the schools to community service agencies electronically, and making certain that libraries are equipped for conducting research and accessing electronic databases.

Teachers Teachers must have the primary voice in what technology should be purchased. Vendors are eager to negotiate with administrators on large-scale purchases with special price breaks on big sales, but teachers must be assured that what they are getting is what they need and want. Teachers must be clear about what they wish to accomplish with their students and not be put off by vendor statements that what they want cannot be done. It may not be possible with the technology one vendor wishes to sell, but it may be possible with another vendor's wares.

The hardware decision is not the most important question confronting teachers. Instructional questions are more important; hardware and software decisions follow decisions about what to teach and how to teach.

The technology systems schools buy should be open rather than closed, proprietary systems. Open systems allow teachers to add other equipment and features in the future as their experience directs them.

Federal and State Government Both the national and state governments can contribute in important ways—not only by the usual methods of subsidizing school renovations, providing funds for equipment, and supporting professional training for teachers, but also by using regulatory authority to make certain schools are served well. Many of the telecommunication companies are urging changes in laws and regulations that will enable them to broaden services to customers and enhance their profits. Both federal and state governments must make certain that the rules are written in ways that schools are treated fairly and can obtain services at prices they can afford. Changes in laws concerning copyright protection should also be undertaken with the interests of schools in mind. States can rewrite rules so that capital funds can be used for equipment purchases and textbook funds for computer software.

Governments must also attend to equity issues resulting from technology use in school. While some schools have bought new equipment using spe-

cial funds targeted to serve poor children, they lack funds to repair that equipment. Inner-city schools often have broken or out-of-date equipment that cannot be fixed or replaced for lack of funds. We already have great disparity between the opportunities afforded the children of poor families as contrasted to those of wealthy families in each state. The equity problem cannot be solved by a single school district; it must be addressed at the level of state and national governments.

The federal government can be a source for research and development support. The states can provide funds that give schools access to the Internet and/or commercial online services. They can also provide incentives for linking the use of technology with school reform measures through subsidizing professional development opportunities for teachers.

Universities Universities should attend to their teacher education programs to make certain that they are providing the technology-capable teacher graduates that schools want to hire. Universities can also begin to make available professional development training by means of distance-learning technology.

Universities ought to be sites for research and development relating to the use of technology in school reform. Universities can also form partnerships with schools to study the process of change that takes place with the introduction and use of technology.

Foundations While large, private foundations have been very active in school reform efforts generally, they have contributed little to the efforts to employ technology for school reform. While it is understandable why foundations want to avoid being drawn into funding the purchase of equipment, they could support other activities, such as technology planning, professional development, and research on the effects of technology use in schools. Foundations might also sponsor technology fairs, bringing teachers and students together across a state or region to celebrate student accomplishments.

Conclusion

It is difficult to imagine conditions more favorable to school reform than those that exist at the present time. Business and government leaders seem intent on maintaining pressure on schools to reform. Teachers, students, parents, and administrators also want change, although not necessarily the same changes desired by national leaders.

Perhaps the most important factor favoring school reform is the impact Information-Age technology is having on all aspects of our culture. To use technology to promote school reform is like flying with a tailwind. Technology can ensure success in school reform. We have only to take advantage of it.

NOTES

Chapter 1

1. SCANS. *What Work Requires of Schools: A SCANS Report for America 2000.* Washington, D.C.: U.S. Department of Labor, June, 1991.

2. *Ibid.*, p. xvii.

3. *Ibid.*, p. xviii.

4. Robert Reich. *The Work of Nations: Preparing Ourselves for 21st Century Capitalism.* New York: Alfred A. Knopf, 1992.

Chapter 2

1. William J. Kohlberg and Foster C. Smith. *Rebuilding America's Workforce: Business Strategies to Close the Competitive Gap.* Homewood, Illinois, Business One, Irwin, 1992, p. 9.

2. Stanley M. Elam, Lowell C. Rose, and Alec M. Gallup. "The 26th Annual Phi Delta Kappa/Gallup Poll of the Public's Attitudes toward the Public Schools." *Phi Delta Kappan,* Vol. 76, No. 1 (September, 1994) 41–56.

3. *Prisoners of Time: A Report of the National Education Commission on Time and Learning.* Washington, D.C.: U.S. Government Printing Office, April, 1994.

4. The report was first published in C. C. Carson, R. M. Huelskamp, and T. D. Woodall. "Perspectives on Education in America: An Annotated Briefing." *The Journal of Educational Research,* Vol. 86, No. 5 (May/June, 1993) 259–311. (Copies of the Sandia report are available for $9.50 from JER, Heldref Publications, 1319 18th St., N.W., Washington, D.C. 200036-1802.) A summary of the report by the same title has been published in the May, 1993 issue of *Phi Delta Kappan.* An account of the politics relating to the publication of the report can be found in Kendrich Frazier. "Perspectives on Education in America: Sandia Study Challenges Misconceptions." *Skeptical Inquirer.* Vol. 18, No. 1 (Fall 1993) 26–31.

5. GED stands for General Equivalency Diploma. This diploma is typically earned by people who are unable to attend regular classes, who pursue independent study, and demonstrate through examination that they have completed the equivalent of a high school education.

6. Clark Kerr, president emeritus, University of California, once commented on the various critics of American education. He said: "Seldom in the course of policy making in the U.S. have so many firm convictions held by so many been based on so little convincing proof."

    Sometimes a "fact that everyone knows to be true" about schools is quoted by one writer after another without checking on its accuracy. One example has occurred with regard to a purported list of the seven most important problems confronting schools in the 1940s (talking, chewing gum, making noise, running in the hall, getting out of turn in line, wearing improper clothing, and not putting paper in wastebaskets) in comparison to problems facing schools in the 1980s (drug abuse, alcohol abuse, pregnancy, suicide, rape, robbery, and assault). These lists, or amended versions of them, have been quoted widely as if they were part of some authoritative study; in fact, they were simply invented by someone to use in a public speech. The idea was picked up in newspaper accounts and thereafter quoted again and again as if the lists were based upon fact. For details, see Barry O'Neil. "The History of a Hoax," *The New York Times Magazine*, March 6, 1994, pp. 46–49.

7. John E. Chubb and Terry M. Moe. *Politics, Markets and America's Schools.* Washington, D.C.: The Brookings Institution, 1990, p. 227.

8. E. P Cubberly. *Public Education in the United States.* Boston: Houghton Mifflin, 1934, pp. 527-8.

9. It may be important to note that this development did not occur in other industrialized countries. For example, in Europe, men have filled the majority of posts in secondary schools and are highly visible in elementary grades as well. The status—and pay—of teachers is higher in countries such as Germany, France, and Switzerland than in the United States.

10. Of course, this was a myth. Until 1954 and the Supreme Court decision in Brown vs. Topeka, Kansas Board of Education, black children attended segregated schools by law. Since 1954 various attempts have been made to integrate schools with varying degrees of success. American public schools may be open to children of all social classes, but students largely attend school with children of similar social class.

11. In 1994 Congress passed legislation called "Goals 2000: Educate America Act." It modified two of the original six goals and added two goals. Goals three and six were modified as below

    3. All students will leave grades 4, 8, and 14 having demonstrated competency in challenging subject matter including English, mathematics, science, *foreign languages, civics and government, economics, arts,* histo-

ry and geography, and every school in America will ensure that all students learn to use their minds well, so that they may be prepared for responsible citizenship, further learning, and productive employment in our modern economy.

6. Every school in the *United States* will be free of drugs, violence, *and the unauthorized presence of firearms and alcohol* and will offer a disciplined environment conducive to learning.

The two additional goals were:

7. The nation's teaching force will have access to programs for the continued improvement of their professional skills and the opportunity to acquire the knowledge and skills needed to instruct and prepare all American students for the next century.

8. Every school will promote partnerships that will increase parental involvement and participation in promoting the social, emotional, and academic growth of children.

12. *America's Choice: high skills or low wages!* The Report of the Commission on the Skills of the American Workforce. Rochester, New York: National Center on Education and the Economy, June 1990.

13. Ray Marshall and Marc Tucker. *Thinking for a Living: Education and the Wealth of Nations.* New York: Basic Books, 1992.

14. Theodore R. Sizer. *Horace's Compromise: The Dilemma of the American High School.* Boston: Houghton Mifflin Company, 1984.

15. Theodore R. Sizer. *Horace's School: Redesigning the American High School.* Boston: Houghton Mifflin Company, 1992.

16. Sizer, *Horace's Compromise*, pp. 207–209.

17. Mary Poplin and Joseph Weeres. *Voices from the Inside: A Report on Schooling from Inside the Classrooms.* Claremont, CA: Institute for Education in Transformation, The Claremont Graduate School, 1992.

18. "Many Schools Are Unsafe, Study Says." *New York Times* (February 2, 1995).

Chapter 3

1. I. P. Pavlov. *Conditioned Reflexes: An Investigation of the Physiological Activity of the Cerebral Cortex.* New York: Dover, 1927, 1960.

B.F. Skinner. *The Behavior of Organisms: An Experimental Analysis.* New York: Appleton, 1938; *Science and Human Behavior.* New York: Macmillan, 1953; *Verbal Behavior.* New York: Appleton, 1957; "The

Science of Learning and the Art of Teaching." *Harvard Education Review*, 24 (1954) 86-97; "Teaching Machines," *Science*, 128 (1958) 969–77.

2. B.S. Bloom. "Mastery Learning" in *Mastery Learning: Theory and Practice*. edited by J. H. Block. New York: Holt, Rinehart, and Winston, 1971; *Every Kid Can: Learning for Mastery*. Washington, D.C.: College/University Press, 1973.

3. Bruno V. Manno. "Outcome-Based Education: Miracle Cure or Plague?" *Hudson (Institute) Briefing Paper*, No. 165, June 1994.

4. Jerome Bruner. *Toward a Theory of Instruction*. New York: W.W. Norton, 1966, p. 44.

5. Howard Gardner. *Frames of Mind: The Theory of Multiple Intelligence*. New York: Basic Books, 1983.

6. John Seely Brown, Allan Collins, and Paul Duguid. "Situated Cognition and the Culture of Learning." *Educational Researcher* (January–February, 1989) 32–42.

7. The Cognition and Technology Group at Vanderbilt. "Anchored Instruction and Its Relationship to Situated Cognition." *Educational Researcher* (August-September, 1990) 2–10.

8. There are many sources on constructivism. One book, focused especially on constructivism and its relationship to instruction, is *Constructivism and the Technology of Instruction: A Conversation*, edited by Thomas M. Duffy and David H. Jonassen. Hillsdale, New Jersey: Lawrence Erlbaum Associates, Publishers, 1992. A book aimed at school applications of constructivism is Jacqueline Grennon Brooks and Martin G. Brooks. *In Search of Understanding: The Case for Constructivist Classrooms*. Alexandria, VA.: Association for Supervision and Curriculum Development, 1993.

9. The origins of these quotations are a mystery to me. They were given to me by someone who originally read them on electronic mail but did not transfer information about the original source. Thus, they can only be cited as "anonymous."

10. *Learner-Centered Psychological Principles: Guidelines for School Design and Reform*. APA Task Force on Psychology and Education and the Mid-Continent Regional Education Laboratory (McREL), January 1993.

11. Richard E. Clark. "Reconsidering Research on Learning from Media." *Review of Educational Research*, Vol. 53, No. 4. (Winter 1983) 445.

12. One place where the debate has been carried on publicly and recently is in the journal *Educational Technology Research and Development*. See

Volume 42, Numbers 2 and 3, 1994 for several articles containing arguments on this issue.

Chapter 4

1. Karen Sheingold. "Restructuring for Learning with Technology: The Potential for Synergy" in *Restructuring for Learning with Technology*, edited by Karen Sheingold and Marc Tucker. New York: Center for Technology in Education, Bank Street College of Education and National Center on Education and the Economy, 1990, p. 9.

2. Establishing precise figures regarding the availability and use of technology is a reckless enterprise. Even when data are gathered carefully and systematically, the numbers become quickly out-of-date. The reader should judge my figures as "best estimates." In arriving at these estimates, I drew heavily upon data compiled by Barbara Means, *et al., Using Technology to Support Education Reform.* Washington, D.C.: U.S. Department of Education, 1993, and data assembled for me by Media Management Services, Inc., which drew upon several databases available to the firm.

3. "Integrated Learning Systems: What Does the Research Say?" *The Computing Teacher* (February 1995) 7–10.

4. The report on the ACOT project was based upon an article by David Dwyer. "Apple Classroom of Tomorrow: What We've Learned." *Educational Leadership.* Vol. 51, No. 7 (April 1994) 4–10.

5. *Report on the Effectiveness of Technology in Schools 1990-1994.* Washington, D.C.: Software Publishers Association, 1994.

6. Means, *op. cit.,* p. 1.

7. *Ibid,* pp. 35–36

Chapter 5

1. The description of Mel Levin was based upon an article called "The Energizer." *Electronic Learning* (September, 1994) 40–42.

2. The description of Bill Burrall was based upon an article by Janet Coburn, that appeared in *Technology and Learning,* 1993.

3. The material on Sherry Clark came from the same article by Janet Coburn.

4. David A. Bennett and D. Thomas King. "The Saturn School of Tomorrow." *Educational Leadership* (May 1991) 41–44.

5. The description of the ACT Academy is based upon my own visit to the school and unpublished materials about the school provided by its director, Linda Farley.

6. The description of the Christopher Columbus School is based upon personal interviews, newspaper articles, and documents provided by school officials, including the evaluation of the first year of Bell Atlantic support.

7. The description is based upon a visit to the community and material supplied by the Forest Hills Public School.

8. The description is based upon various published accounts and documents provided by school officials.

Chapter 6

1. Geoffrey H. Fletcher. Texas Education Agency, Division of Educational Technology. Quoted in the National Governors Association *Task Force on Technology Report*, p. 125.

2. Lewis Perelman. *School's Out: Hyperlearning, the New Technology, and the End of Education.* New York: William Morrow and Company, Inc., 1992.

3. Michael G. Fullan and Matthew B. Miles. "Getting Reform Right: What Works and What Doesn't." *Phi Delta Kappan* (June 1992) 745–52.

4. *School Facilities: Condition of America's Schools* (GAO/HEHS-95-61, February 1, 1995).

5. *School Facilities: America's Schools Not Designed or Equipped for the 21st Century* (GAO/HEHS-95-95, April 4, 1995).

ABOUT THE AUTHOR

Howard D. Mehlinger is the director of Indiana University's Center for Excellence in Education, a research and development center whose mission is to explore appropriate applications of technology in education. He is also a professor of Education and History and co-directs the Institute for the Study of Russian Education at Indiana University.

Mehlinger's entire professional career has been marked by educational reform. He began as a high school world history and American government teacher and football coach at Lawrence (Kansas) High School. During the decade he taught in Lawrence, he was a pilot teacher for new curriculum materials in foreign relations, world history, and Asian studies; he developed college-level courses for high school seniors in American government and a modern history of China and Japan; and directed a social studies team teaching project that was emulated by other schools.

In 1963 he became co-director of the Social Studies Curriculum Development Center at Carnegie Mellon University, where he wrote curriculum materials for a ninth-grade course in comparative politics. In 1964 he was appointed associate director of the North Central Association's Foreign Relations Project, an effort to improve the teaching of international studies in American schools.

In 1965 he moved to Indiana University where he successively served as deputy director of the Inter-University Committee on Travel Grants, a consortium of American universities created to promote graduate study in the USSR and countries of Eastern Europe; director of the High School Curriculum Center in Government, a federally funded project that led to the development of a new high school course called *American Political Behavior;* director of the Social Studies Development Center, a research and development center that produced a variety of innovative programs for social studies teachers and students; dean of the Indiana University School of Education, where he provided leadership for reforms in teacher education; co-director of the Institute for the Study of Russian Education, which is assisting with educational reform in Russia; and director of the Center for Excellence in Education.

During his career of more than 40 years he has been fortunate to participate in many educational reforms, including some that he initiated. The current school reform movement may not be the last he will experience, but it is the one he believes has the best opportunity for long-term success.